# Money, Lies and the Church
What the Bible really says about financial giving.

By Bruce Kurtzer

© - 2022 – Bruce Kurtzer
Permission is granted to use this book or portions of it for teaching and Bible studies, providing it is done so freely and without any admission charges or other fees.
Any other use needs the permission of the author.
www.simplechurch.com.au
ISBN 978-0-9953620-1-7
First printing 2022

IMPORTANT NOTES WHEN READING THIS BOOK:
- The author's conviction is that the church is the gathering of all believers and not a building or property used for such a gathering. However, the word 'church' used in this book often refers to the traditional understanding of church, that being a building where Christians gather, normally on a Sunday. Sometimes the author refers to it as 'institutionalised church' or 'traditional church'.
- Unless otherwise stated, all Scripture is quoted from the NASB Strong's Bible Text (Lockman Edition)

With thanks to my wife and family for their support.
Dedicated to all that are seeking the truth.

**About the author**
Bruce Kurtzer has served as a Pastor for many years within a formal church setting. With a desire to see the church like in the New Testament, he now serves the Body of Christ, predominately through the simple organic church movement.

His unique style of ministry opens up the truth in a way that can be understood by people of all ages. Through this book, he shares his heart and journey of being a secret giver, while exposing biblical truths about giving. He writes this book to introduce people to the joy and freedom of biblical financial giving.

He can be contacted through his website:
www.simplechurch.com.au

*'No one can serve two masters; for either he will hate the one and love the other, or he will be devoted to one and despise the other. You cannot serve God and wealth.'*
*Matthew 6:24*

*"Woe to you, blind guides, who say, 'Whoever swears by the temple, that is nothing; but whoever swears by the gold of the temple is obligated.' [17] You fools and blind men! Which is more important, the gold or the temple that sanctified the gold?*
*Matthew 23:16-17*

*'This is a faithful saying: If a man desires the position of a bishop, he desires a good work. [2] A bishop then must be blameless, the husband of one wife, temperate, sober-minded, of good behavior, hospitable, able to teach; [3] not given to wine, not violent, not greedy for money, but gentle, not quarrelsome, <u>not covetous</u>;'*
*1 Timothy 3:1-3*

**Covetousness is greed, contentment is freedom.**

## Contents

Preface .................................................................... 11
Introduction ........................................................... 13
1. How does God see money? ............................. 17
2. Generous giving or obligated giving ................ 23
3. Abusive giving – The widow's last coins ........ 33
4. Let your giving be done in secret ................... 39
5. The sermon before the offering ..................... 43
6. Don't give to receive more money ................. 47
7. Tithing, the financial giving of 10% ............... 55
8. What Malachi says about tithing .................... 69
9. The Melchizedek argument ............................ 77
10. Summarizing tithing ...................................... 81
11. Turning over the money changers' tables ..... 83
12. The business of the church ........................... 91
13. Who to give to? .............................................. 99
14. Exposing the prosperity doctrine ............... 105
15. Covetousness versus contentment ............ 119

## Preface

For years I was convinced by many of the teachings of the church about financial giving. Teachings like giving a tithe (10%) of all your income; sowing your money into the church to receive more money back; giving regular first-fruit offerings.
I tithed and gave generous offerings; I sowed financial seeds expecting a return; I generously supported building programs, missionaries, and charities. This is difficult for me to confess because I love to give unnoticed and not draw attention to myself, which is what I freely do today.

As someone who likes to give anonymously without strings attached it seems unusual to write about it. It was never my intention to write a book about giving money and the teachings of the church around it. However, I discovered new freedom and joy by honouring the biblical principles about giving, and it is this that I would love you, the reader, to experience as well: freedom from obligated tithing and compelling offerings and joy from knowing that you have secretly contributed to help meet someone else's needs.

Yes, I did believe many of the financial principles that the church taught me, and as a preacher, I even preached some of them myself. While some held value and truth, others were false and deceptive. I was unaware of the journey I would go on by studying the Scriptural references about finances. Along this journey, I have considered different views from denominations, cultures, church traditions, and individuals. I have attempted to weigh them up with Scripture.

My motive as writer is for you as reader to learn about the freedom and joy of anonymous, generous, free-willed giving; breaking away from unbiblical, obligated giving. You will be able to do this by being prepared to unlearn what you know and to relearn the principles through studying and obeying Scripture. I pray that this book will be a useful guide in doing so.

Are you willing to examine and obey Scripture in the area of financial giving?

To get the most out of this book, be prepared to go on a journey similar to mine, through Scripture; a journey of unlearning what you thought you knew in order to relearn what the Bible says. If you are prepared to begin this journey, start with a blank canvas: with no preconceived ideas, just the Bible as your guide and the Holy Spirit as your teacher. That's what I did, and this book contains the notes of my discoveries along the way. Some were things I knew that became revived and refreshed, others were new and fresh, straight from the Spirit of God.

## Introduction

To some of you, the message I want to transmit through this book may be challenging or controversial, to others it may get many 'amens', but do not believe it or anything I am about to say. Do not believe anything your pastor/leader says or has said. Learn it yourself from the Bible, allow the Holy Spirit to be your teacher. While my opinion and the opinion of others may guide you, the Holy Spirit is your true teacher, so be prepared to examine Scripture and be taught by Him.

This book may present some theology that grinds what you currently know. You may not agree with everything in this book, but please do not let that cause you to draw judgement on others that disagree with your views. This book is not the Bible even though it contains many verses. This book is to be used as a map; a guide for you to study Scripture yourself regarding finances and the church.

> *'Now these were more noble-minded than those in Thessalonica, for they received the word with great eagerness, examining the Scriptures daily to see whether these things were so.'*
> Acts 17:11

In Acts 17:10-15, the people in Berea welcomed the teaching that came from Paul and Silas, but they were commended for examining Scripture daily to see if what Paul and Silas were saying was true. My prayer for you is that you would do the same while reading this book.

While there have been some good and valuable things taught through the church about finances, I have also observed some false and deceptive teachings and practices around the topic. Some of which I have observed include:

- At a particular Christian conference, they ran a leader-board that ranked people's individual givings from most to least.
- A youth who attended a Christian youth meeting for the first time, was taught that they needed to give 10% (a tithe) of all their money.
- I remember being taught if I didn't give a tithe, I allowed the accuser (the devil) access to my money and more than 10% would be lost and wasted. I figured that God must remove His blessing if we didn't tithe.
- I've heard the televangelists promise that God would answer and intercede for my needs if I simply sent him some money or purchased his product.
- An offering message I heard once taught me that we must choose to sow our finances into good soil, and that good soil is their church.
- I remember a preacher holding up an offering bucket and asking, 'Who wants their increase?'
- And let's not forget the most common teaching: when we give we sow a seed, and as such, we should

expect a financial return.

It was back in the late 1990s in Australia when I first observed the practice of sharing a message about financial giving before receiving every offering. It seemed to have started in Pentecostal and Charismatic churches, but soon more churches were doing the same. While some of the messages have presented elements of truth, other messages are purposely misleading, anti-biblical and just a way to beg for money.

**I remember asking *'why do we need to have a message about financial giving every week?'***
I attended pastors' conferences and again they would present a message about financial giving before they received the offering. Being a room full of pastors and leaders, you would assume that they knew about giving.

Back then, I was pastoring a church and there was an unwritten expectation to follow the tradition and share a message about giving before the offering. Yes, I did do it, many times. Eventually, I tried to change the weekly message about financial giving to a message about evangelism and a challenge for everyone to share their faith. This didn't go well with some people, and I wonder how different the church would be today if it focused more on encouraging people to share their faith rather than to give their money.

Let us look at what Scripture says regarding some of the abuses and wrong teaching about financial giving but let me make it clear; this book is <u>NOT</u> an anti-giving message. It is a message that encourages Christians to be generous in their financial giving and to give biblically and with the right attitude.

Before you progress any further, stop and pray. Open your heart and use this book to aid you in examining Scripture on the subject of finances and the church. Some chapters will give you great biblical principles about financial giving, while others will expose some of the lies taught about financial giving, tithing and prosperity.

## 1. How does God see money?

Have you ever asked yourself, 'what is money to God?'
God indeed blesses us, but why would He bless us with money when He has things far greater than that? The blessings He has for us, money could never buy. Yet many today simply believe God will supply them with more money.
Money belongs to our worldly economic system.

> '"Shall we pay or shall we not pay?" But He, knowing their hypocrisy, said to them, "Why are you testing Me? Bring Me a denarius to look at." [16] They brought one. And He said to them, "Whose likeness and inscription is this?" And they said to Him, "Caesar's." [17] And Jesus said to them, "Render to Caesar the things that are Caesar's, and to God the things that are God's." And they were amazed at Him.'
> Mark 12:15-17

Jesus identified money as belonging to Caesar because on it, it was Caesar's image and therefore it belonged to him. However, He also commanded us to render to God the things that are God's. What are the things of God? Is it not the things with God's image on them? Would it not be His creation; the earth, the heavens, the universe, mankind? It all belongs to God.
Money is man-made and only has value in the man-made economic system, yet we put so much focus on

it. The money a church has or the money an individual has often determines how successful they are, but that is only a man-made secular measurement of success.

**Money, in God's eyes, is not a measurement of success.**

While it is true that God blessed some of the Old Testament saints like Solomon and Abraham with wealth, their focus was never on wealth. Solomon asked for wisdom, not money; and Abraham was promised to be the father of many nations – a greater blessing than money. Both Solomon and Abraham's focus was on eternal things rather than perishable wealth.

No amount of money can ever compare with the promise of eternal life. God has already given us everything and He owes us nothing.

*'No one can serve two masters; for either he will hate the one and love the other, or he will be devoted to one and despise the other. You cannot serve God and wealth.'*
Matthew 6:24

*'Listen, my beloved brethren: did not God choose the poor of this world to be rich in faith and heirs of the kingdom which He promised to those who love Him?'*
James 2:5

What is money to God? Is it not simply metal and paper with the image of a man on it? Even in a cashless society, money is simply a way to fund and resource a man-made economic system. For us, as people that live in such a system, it becomes a resource for provision, even though God Himself promises to be our resource.

> 'Do not worry then, saying, "What will we eat?" or "What will we drink?" or "What will we wear for clothing?" *32* For the Gentiles eagerly seek all these things; for your heavenly Father knows that you need all these things. *33* But seek first His kingdom and His righteousness, and all these things will be added to you.'
> Matthew 6:31-33

> 'I have been young and now I am old, Yet I have not seen the righteous forsaken Or his descendants begging bread.'
> Psalms 37:25

While money is one of the ways in which God can provide for our resources, it is not the only way. He can provide for us in so many other ways. Remember how He provided for the Israelites in the Old Testament. They spent 40 years in the desert and God miraculously provided for their every need.

> 'Then the Lord said to Moses, "Behold, I will rain bread from heaven for you; and the people shall go out and gather a day's portion every day, that I may test them, whether or not they will walk in My instruction. ⁵ On the sixth day, when they prepare what they bring in, it will be twice as much as they gather daily."'
> Exodus 16:4-5

> 'I have heard the grumblings of the sons of Israel; speak to them, saying, "At twilight you shall eat meat, and in the morning you shall be filled with bread; and you shall know that I am the Lord your God." ¹³ So it came about at evening that the quails came up and covered the camp, and in the morning there was a layer of dew around the camp.'
> Exodus 16:12-13

There are also many other examples in the Old Testament of God providing without using money as a resource. In this one example in Exodus, not only did He provide for their need, but He also had to deal with people's greed or unbelief. He had promised to provide for them daily, but some people took too much, and their extravagance rotted overnight.

> 'But they did not listen to Moses, and some left part of it until morning, and it bred worms and became foul; and Moses was angry with them.'
> Exodus 16:20

God providing for people without using money as a resource is also seen in the New Testament. The feeding of the 5,000 by using a few fish and loaves of bread is just one example.

> 'When it was evening, the disciples came to Him and said, "This place is desolate and the hour is already late; so send the crowds away, that they may go into the villages and buy food for themselves." [16] But Jesus said to them, "They do not need to go away; you give them something to eat!"'
> Matthew 14:15-16

The disciples planned to send the people away so that they could buy (with money) food, but Jesus provided the food miraculously.

**The disciples' focus was on a natural provision; Jesus's focus was on a miraculous provision.**

God promises to provide for us, but He doesn't necessarily do it through money. Our focus should be on Him as our provider and not on how He will provide. We need to know though that He is the provider of all our needs, but not our greed.

## 2. Generous giving or obligated giving

Some people may not like to hear this, but throughout the Bible, giving has always been very much a part of a believer's life.
Several times in the book of Acts we find that they were selling their possessions and giving the proceeds away to help people in need.

> 'And all those who had believed were together and had all things in common; [45] and they began selling their property and possessions and were sharing them with all, as anyone might have need.'
> Acts 2:44-45

> 'For there was not a needy person among them, for all who were owners of land or houses would sell them and bring the proceeds of the sales [35] and lay them at the apostles' feet, and they would be distributed to each as any had need.'
> Acts 4:34-35

Imagine if the church was like that today. Just dream with me. Unfortunately, some institutionalised churches take up large offerings to pay for their building; their wages; to purchase 'necessary' stage lighting and effects, and a range of things they 'need' to run a 'relevant' service. All while a poor widow struggles to pay her rent, power and food.

Would Jesus be delighted with financially giving to a church for its needs while leaving the individual in need to struggle and go hungry?

There seems to be a major difference between giving as seen in the New Testament and the giving that is often promoted in churches today. We see a similar difference between Old Testament giving and New Testament giving.

In the Old Testament giving was obligated; sacrifices, tithes, offerings were compulsory for people, whereas in the New Testament giving was expected but optional. In the Old Testament they gave out of obedience to the law, whereas in the New Testament the motive should be love and compassion.

Even though some New Testament Scripture is very strong in the direction to give, it is always motivated by love and compassion.

> *'But whoever has the world's goods, and sees his brother in need and closes his heart against him, how does the love of God abide in him?'*
> *1 John 3:17*

> *'If someone says, "I love God," and hates his brother, he is a liar; for the one who does not love his brother whom he has seen, cannot love God whom he has not seen. 21 And this commandment we have from Him, that the one who loves God should love his brother also.'*
> *1 John 4:20-21*

Much of the giving we see in churches today seem to be motivated by obligation rather than out of love and compassion.

We witness some of that love and compassion in the church in the book of Acts when they gave to ensure that none of them went without. I wonder how the world saw this crazy bunch of believers in Jesus (the early church) as they gave to make sure that nobody among them had a need, and that everyone was cared for. The sense of community they portrayed must have been such a powerful witness to the love of Christ.

In comparison, today's church is often seen by the world as rich and money-hungry. How different the image of the church was back then compared to how it is often seen today. It seems more concerned about maintaining buildings and having an image of prosperity than caring for a person who is struggling and in need.

Our giving has missed the New Testament mark, as it is often not given freely and generously but out of compulsion and obligation. There is a big difference between giving because we have been told to and giving because we want to. No matter how much money we give, it is not generous or a sacrifice if we have been forced to give it. Forcing someone to give could be described as theft.

**Generous giving is not necessarily giving a lot or making sacrifices.**
Someone wealthy can easily give a greater amount than someone poorer. As for sacrifice, it takes less for the poor to give everything they own and not leave anything for themselves, but is this sacrifice what God expects, or is it foolishness? We will answer that in the next chapter.

What, therefore, is generous giving? True generous giving is not done out of coercion or forced obligation. Generous giving is when we choose to give, not because we must, but because we desire to. **Generous giving is motivated by love and compassion whereas obligated giving is motivated by duty and obedience.**

### Motivation

*'And He also told this parable to some people who trusted in themselves that they were righteous, and viewed others with contempt: ¹⁰ "Two men went up into the temple to pray, one a Pharisee and the other a tax collector. ¹¹ The Pharisee stood and was praying this to himself: "God, I thank You that I am not like other people: swindlers, unjust, adulterers, or even like this tax collector. ¹² I fast twice a week; I pay tithes of all that I get." ¹³ But the tax collector, standing some distance away, was even unwilling to lift up his eyes to heaven, but was beating his breast, saying, "God, be merciful to me, the sinner!" ¹⁴ I tell you, this man went*

> to his house justified rather than the other; for everyone who exalts himself will be humbled, but he who humbles himself will be exalted.'
> Luke 18:9-14

In this parable, the Pharisee stood and boastfully acknowledged that he is more blessed than others because he fasts twice a week and pays tithes on everything he receives. Alongside the Pharisee was a tax collector. He didn't even mention if he gave anything, but just pleaded for mercy.

I have seen some television preachers like this Pharisee, boastfully claiming about how blessed they are, telling people that by tithing they will be blessed like them as well. The Pharisee and the tax collector had different motivations – one was prideful, the other repentant and humble. Jesus justified the latter and condemned the other.

## **Sacrifice**

Sacrifice is not an amount, but rather a proportion of the total.

We tend to give more sacrificially to those close to us because sacrificial giving is a sign that we truly love and care for someone. God Himself made the ultimate sacrifice when he gave His Son for us. He did it to help us because He truly loves us.

> 'For God so loved the world, that He gave His only begotten Son, that whoever believes in Him shall not

*perish, but have eternal life.'*
*John 3:16*

**The early disciples practised sacrificial giving with genuine love, concern, and compassion for each other.**

*'And the congregation of those who believed were of one heart and soul; and not one of them claimed that anything belonging to him was his own, but all things were common property to them. $^{33}$ And with great power the apostles were giving testimony to the resurrection of the Lord Jesus, and abundant grace was upon them all. $^{34}$ For there was not a needy person among them, for all who were owners of land or houses would sell them and bring the proceeds of the sales $^{35}$ and lay them at the apostles' feet, and they would be distributed to each as any had need. $^{36}$ Now Joseph, a Levite of Cyprian birth, who was also called Barnabas by the apostles (which translated means Son of Encouragement), $^{37}$ and who owned a tract of land, sold it and brought the money and laid it at the apostles' feet.'*
*Acts 4:32-37*

**Immediately after this, they witnessed two people drop dead because of their deception.**

'But a man named Ananias, with his wife Sapphira, sold a piece of property, [2] and kept back some of the price for himself, with his wife's full knowledge, and bringing a portion of it, he laid it at the apostles' feet. [3] But Peter said, "Ananias, why has Satan filled your heart to lie to the Holy Spirit and to keep back some of the price of the land? [4] While it remained unsold, did it not remain your own? And after it was sold, was it not under your control? Why is it that you have conceived this deed in your heart? You have not lied to men but to God." [5] And as he heard these words, Ananias fell down and breathed his last; and great fear came over all who heard of it. [6] The young men got up and covered him up, and after carrying him out, they buried him.
[7] Now there elapsed an interval of about three hours, and his wife came in, not knowing what had happened. [8] And Peter responded to her, "Tell me whether you sold the land for such and such a price?" And she said, "Yes, that was the price." [9] Then Peter said to her, "Why is it that you have agreed together to put the Spirit of the Lord to the test? Behold, the feet of those who have buried your husband are at the door, and they will carry you out as well." [10] And immediately she fell at his feet and breathed her last, and the young men came in and found her dead, and they carried her out and buried her beside her husband. [11] And great fear came over the whole church, and over all who heard of these things.'

Acts 5:1-11

Ananias and Sapphira did NOT drop dead because they didn't give enough; their judgement was because they lied about their giving. They took pride in giving the entire amount that they received for their land even though they held some back. The key verse is verse 4, which indicates it was up to them how much they gave.

> *'"While it remained unsold, did it not remain your own? And after it was sold, was it not under your control? Why is it that you have conceived this deed in your heart? You have not lied to men but to God."'*
> Acts 5:4

The profit from selling their land was theirs to do what they wanted. They didn't have to give it, but they chose to lie and claim that they gave it all.

Just like the Pharisee, the tax collector, Ananias and Sapphira, we too have a choice:
- We can pridefully give like the Pharisee.
- We can give out of obligation like in the Old Testament, which in essence is not generous giving at all.
- We can dishonestly give like Ananias and Sapphira.
- We can practice New Testament generous giving, which is directed by God and will sometimes be a bigger sacrifice but will always be motivated out of love and compassion.

I pray that you will practice the latter, for surely that is generous giving; giving as you are directed by God and <u>NOT</u> by man, a service or a program.

## 3. Abusive giving – The widow's last coins

Unfortunately, like almost everything, the requirement to freely and generously give has been abused by mankind. This abuse can be seen in the account of the widow's offering.

> 'And He sat down opposite the treasury, and began observing how the people were putting money into the treasury; and many rich people were putting in large sums. $^{42}$ A poor widow came and put in two small copper coins, which amount to a cent. $^{43}$ Calling His disciples to Him, He said to them, "Truly I say to you, this poor widow put in more than all the contributors to the treasury; $^{44}$ for they all put in out of their surplus, but she, out of her poverty, put in all she owned, all she had to live on."'
> Mark 12:41-44

> 'And He looked up and saw the rich putting their gifts into the treasury. $^2$ And He saw a poor widow putting in two small copper coins. $^3$ And He said, "Truly I say to you, this poor widow put in more than all of them; $^4$ for they all out of their surplus put into the offering; but she out of her poverty put in all that she had to live on."'
> Luke 21:1-4

The account of this widow putting all she had to live on in the offering has been preached as an illustration of generous, sacrificial giving. However, when we have a closer look at the account and put it in context, we discover more condemnation about an abusive system, than a command to sacrificial giving.

We observe that the receiving of the offering was a very public and visual show. Jesus and others in the crowd saw the large sums the rich were putting in. Some of them may have given with such pride and showmanship. This contradicts many of the sound, biblical giving principles that we will address in this book. It was an unethical and religious system that made a public show out of giving. Those putting in their large amounts would've been expecting a compliment. The same people probably mocked the widow's small offering. But Jesus brought attention to those few small coins and credited the widow with giving more than anyone else.

> 'Calling His disciples to Him, He said to them, "Truly I say to you, this poor widow put in more than all the contributors to the treasury; [44] for they all put in out of their surplus, but she, out of her poverty, put in all she owned, all she had to live on."'
> Mark 12:43-44

While Jesus did tell His disciples that she gave more, there is never any mention that we should follow the widow's example.

Jesus also drew attention to the fact that *"she put in*

*all she owned, all she had to live on."* She had nothing left. Does God expect us to give all our money and leave nothing to provide for ourselves?

Money is a man-made system to provide for our basic human needs. These needs exist for every human and out of love we should be happy to contribute to meeting other people's needs. However, is it foolishness or faith to give it all away and not provide for our own needs; not to use it for what it was designed for?

*'But if anyone does not provide for his own, and especially for those of his household, he has denied the faith and is worse than an unbeliever.'*
1 Timothy 5:8

Timothy tells us that we deny the faith and are worse than an unbeliever if we do not provide for our household.

So, is the widow's offering a positive illustration of sacrificial giving, or is it a judgement and condemnation on a system that had no concern for the practical provisions of the widow? Looking at the verses before and after would indicate that it is the latter, that it is not about giving but about judgement on a religious system that is robbing the poor. Just look at the verses directly before in Mark's account.

> [38] 'In His teaching He was saying: "Beware of the scribes who like to walk around in long robes, and like respectful greetings in the market places, [39] and chief seats in the synagogues and places of honor at banquets, [40] who devour widows' houses, and for appearance's sake offer long prayers; these will receive greater condemnation."'
> Mark 12:38-40

These verses are addressing a prideful religious system that desires to look good to the secular world. It is interesting how it even mentions that they 'devour widows' houses'. Is this not what happened just a few verses later when this widow gave everything she had? This is very similar to what we see in some churches today when people are told to give before paying their bills and providing for their basic needs.

How would you feel seeing a widow give all she has into a religious system and then go home hungry? Does God want a widow to give away all her money so that she is not provided for? This would be a contradiction with so many other Scriptures that command us to look after widows.

> 'A father of the fatherless and a judge for the widows,
> Is God in His holy habitation.'
> Psalms 68:5

> *"'Cursed is he who distorts the justice due an alien, orphan, and widow."'*
> *And all the people shall say, "Amen."'*
> *Deuteronomy 27:19*

> *'Pure and undefiled religion in the sight of our God and Father is this: to visit orphans and widows in their distress, and to keep oneself unstained by the world.'*
> *James 1:27*

> *'Kindness to the poor is a loan to the Lord, and He will give a reward to the lender.'*
> *Proverbs 19:17*

The widow that gave the offering of the two coins may have given it sincerely and with good intentions, even though it was likely given under the pressure to be seen that she was giving something. What Jesus addressed though, was the religious system that would coerce and pressure people to give to the system, with no concern about the basic needs and provisions of the people.

It was an abuse of giving, it was unethical, it was compassionless. Unfortunately, we still see it happening today with some prosperity teachers telling people to give their last few dollars instead of paying their bills. Others have suggested to make a donation that takes your credit card to its limit and see God return it tenfold. These are abuses that should have no place in the church.

Giving is biblical, but abusing is not. The widow's offering is one example of why we need to understand the truth and expose some lies about giving.

## 4. Let your giving be done in secret

In the previous chapter we saw how the widow was caught in a system where giving was made very public and visual. New Testament giving is not meant to be a public display but rather it should be done secretively.

> 'Beware of practicing your righteousness before men to be noticed by them; otherwise you have no reward with your Father who is in heaven.
> ² "So when you give to the poor, do not sound a trumpet before you, as the hypocrites do in the synagogues and in the streets, so that they may be honored by men. Truly I say to you, they have their reward in full. ³ But when you give to the poor, do not let your left hand know what your right hand is doing, ⁴ so that your giving will be in secret; and your Father who sees what is done in secret will reward you."'
> Matthew 6:1-4

In Matthew 6 Jesus endorsed financial giving, but commands that such giving be done in secret. When He says, 'when you give to the poor' it is an expectation that you would be giving to the poor. He follows this with 'do not let your left hand know what your right hand is doing' this is a command that it should be done secretly.

Some years ago, I made a decision not to participate in giving through text messages, or named envelopes, or by purchasing a brick, seat or other items with my name on them. I decided to give as anonymously as possible. While some may say 'that's extreme' or that I'm not up with modern technology, my decision to give this way was made to align myself with scriptural giving.

Matthew chapter 6 tells us that our left hand is not meant to know what our right hand is doing. This shows how anonymously our giving is meant to be. Both hands are part of the same body, always working together. They work closely together and in co-operation, so not letting your left hand know what your right hand is doing means it needs to be a very private action.

The church has been very creative with some of its fundraising and giving programs, but not all of these enable the option to give in secret. Many online platforms for giving require you to give your name and other details and there is no option for anonymous giving. While some people may like to give their details so they can claim what they're giving on their tax, others may not be interested in claiming tax benefits and simply want to give anonymously, in obedience to Scripture. While I understand that your giving may never be completely anonymous and there is often a way to track people's details, I love the challenge of attempting to give as secretly as possible.

I am not condemning or criticising people that give by means that are not anonymous. It is about your motive. If you're giving to make yourself look good and generous; if you're giving to earn a reward, then your motive is wrong and you are NOT giving scripturally. This is exactly what Matthew chapter 6 talks about.

> *'Beware of practicing your righteousness before men to be noticed by them; otherwise you have no reward with your Father who is in heaven.'*
> Matthew 6:1

Giving to be noticed by men gets no reward from our Father in heaven. The word 'men' here includes everyone and is not based on gender. It includes all the televangelists who promise they will recognise you if you give to them. God's reward and favour is not determined by how generously you have given to a recognised tele-evangelist.

> *2 '"So when you give to the poor, do not sound a trumpet before you, as the hypocrites do in the synagogues and in the streets, so that they may be honored by men. Truly I say to you, they have their reward in full. 3 But when you give to the poor, do not let your left hand know what your right hand is doing, 4 so that your giving will be in secret; and your Father*

*who sees what is done in secret will reward you."'*
Matthew 6:2-4

Your giving is always personal; between you and God. Your Father (God) who sees what you have done in secret, will reward you in His time. While some may preach that the reward for financial giving is a financial return, God's reward can be far more valuable and eternal than man-made money. A reward shouldn't be our motive for giving.

## 5. The sermon before the offering

*'Each one must do just as he has purposed in his heart, not grudgingly or under compulsion, for God loves a cheerful giver.'*
*2 Corinthians 9:7*

This Scripture in 2 Corinthians 9:7 tells us that God loves a cheerful giver. He loves it when we freely give cheerfully, as we purposed in our hearts. However, it also warns us about being compelled to give and giving grudgingly.

The word compulsion means to make it feel necessary, compulsory, to be obliged. In some areas, compulsion isn't bad. For example, in Luke 14:23 we are told to compel people to come in, this is a good compulsion.

However, when it comes to money, 2 Corinthians 9:7 tells us not to give grudgingly or when we are being compelled to.

It is a common practice today in many modern churches to have an offering message; a message about giving just before receiving the tithes and offerings. Some may argue that such a message is teaching about biblical financial giving, but why do we need to teach people about financial giving every week? Why don't we teach people about sharing the gospel with their neighbours every week?

While I have heard some good messages about giving, I have also heard many offering messages that are not biblical and are simply a way to compel people to give, and often with an attitude of receiving.

I have talked with people that feel second-class and uncomfortable in church as they don't have the means to give more, and according to what they've been taught, a lack of means represents a lack of faith; a lack of God's blessing or favour. But God's blessing and favour cannot be bought and is not based on how much we financially give.

> 'Blessed be the God and Father of our Lord Jesus Christ, who has blessed us with every spiritual blessing in the heavenly places in Christ.'
> Ephesians 1:3

Unfortunately, many of these offering messages come down to begging people to give more. I have witnessed this, and I have even seen the offering collected for a second time as there wasn't enough collected the first time.

So what is the real purpose of having an offering message; is it to teach giving, or is it to increase the amount collected through the offering?
It is common knowledge among pastors that having offering messages often results in larger finances received through the offering. Is this a bad thing? Is it

wrong to receive a large offering? Not at all. But to use compulsion and guilt to get that money is.

I decided not to give to any organisation or church that compels me to give. I will not give under compulsion. If I hear a good offering message that has compelled me to give, I do not give to the church, event or ministry that has compelled me. Rather, after the service I find a needy person and give to them. I encourage you to do the same.

## 6. Don't give to receive more money

The most common theme in offering messages is sowing and reaping, or in other words, giving money so that you can receive more money. This is called the *sowing and reaping principle*.

> 'So I thought it necessary to urge the brethren that they would go on ahead to you and arrange beforehand your previously promised bountiful gift, so that the same would be ready as a bountiful gift and not affected by covetousness.
> [6] Now this I say, he who sows sparingly will also reap sparingly, and he who sows bountifully will also reap bountifully. [7] Each one must do just as he has purposed in his heart, not grudgingly or under compulsion, for God loves a cheerful giver.'
> 2 Corinthians 9:5-7

In these verses, we find Paul is urging the church to give generously to the saints (vs1). However, verse 5 ends with a word that has been translated as covetousness. Other translations use words such as 'grudging', 'obligation', or 'extortion'. The Greek word for this concept indicates 'greedy desire to have more, covetousness, avarice'.

Today we have people giving with that desire, the desire to have more, not the desire to love and help those in need. Maybe the question we need to ask every giver is *would you still give if there was no* promised return? Would you still give if the promised return was not a natural return but a supernatural one? After all, the natural return will pass away but the supernatural return is eternal.

Maybe next time you feel pressured to give, it is time to check your heart and only give out of love and compassion.

> 'So I thought it necessary to urge the brethren that they would go on ahead to you and arrange beforehand your previously promised bountiful gift, so that the same would be ready as a bountiful gift and not affected by **covetousness**.
> ⁶ Now this I say, he who sows sparingly will also reap sparingly, and he who sows bountifully will also reap bountifully.'
> 2 Corinthians 9:5-6

2 Corinthians 9:6 is often quoted by itself to encourage people to give to receive. This is often done without any mention of the verse before, which speaks of covetousness, greed and a desire to get more. Look at the amplified translation of the Scripture.

> That is why I thought it necessary to urge these brethren to go to you before I do and make arrangements in advance for this bountiful, promised gift of yours, so that it may be ready, not as an extortion [wrung out of you] but as a generous and willing gift.

*⁶ [Remember] this: he who sows sparingly and grudgingly will also reap sparingly and grudgingly, and he who sows generously [that blessings may come to someone] will also reap generously and with blessings.*
*2 Corinthians 9:5-6*

Verse 6 mentions the word 'sow' and aligns the sowing with 'sparing and grudging' and 'generously that blessing may come to someone'.
**It is not talking about what you're sowing but rather how you're sowing it.**
The sowing here is about attitude and a selfless attitude desiring to give to help rather than to receive. This fits in with the context of the verses before and after. When you are giving with the right attitude, the promised reaping will come about. What do we reap? According to verse 10, it is righteousness. The harvest is righteousness.

*'Now He who supplies seed to the sower and bread for food will supply and multiply your seed for sowing and increase the harvest of your righteousness;'*
*2 Corinthians 9:10*

So, what is the seed that we sow? We will find the answer in the parable of the sower, which is often misquoted and used to teach financial giving.
Terms like: 'sowing into good soil', 'sowing seed', 'sowing to reap a good harvest,' have all come from misusing the parable of the sower.
Let's have a look at the parable and get some

answers.

The parable can be found in three gospels (Matthew 13:1-23, Mark 4:1-20, Luke 8:4-15). All three also record Jesus' explanation and He never gives any indication that the parable is about money.
In Luke 8:11 He says, 'Now the parable is this: the seed is the word of God.'

The lesson of the parable is that we are to sow the word of God wherever we go, some will receive it and others will not. The idea of a church being good soil and therefore we should sow into it is not supported at all by this parable. The sower never examined the soil before sowing. You would think that a sower would know to only sow in good soil, not just to scatter seed everywhere. Yet when we understand that the seed is the word of God, we can then understand that the sower (like us) is called to scatter the word of God everywhere.

Two more Scriptures that have been used by some preachers and televangelists to encourage and compel people to give more to receive more are found in Luke 6:38 and Philippians 4:17-19

> *'"Give, and it will be given to you. They will pour into your lap a good measure—pressed down, shaken together, and running over. For by your standard of measure it will be measured to you in return."'*
> *Luke 6:38*

Out of context, some say that if you want to financially receive, pressed down, shaken together and running over, you need to financially give the same way. Yet when we look at the verses before and after (Luke 6:35-42), in its context we see Jesus was never talking about finances in this passage. He was talking about giving mercy and forgiveness to those who appear to be our enemy. He was telling us to be merciful and forgiving to those who may be against us in the same way that we expect God to be merciful and forgiving towards us.

Jesus didn't change His thoughts in the middle of His teaching about mercy and compassion to speak about financial giving and to make a promise about its return.

> *'Not that I seek the gift itself, but I seek for the profit which increases to your account. $^{18}$ But I have received everything in full and have an abundance; I am amply supplied, having received from Epaphroditus what you have sent, a fragrant aroma, an acceptable sacrifice, well-pleasing to God. $^{19}$ And my God will supply all your needs according to His riches in glory in Christ Jesus.'*
> Philippians 4:17-19

In these verses, Paul was saying he wasn't seeking the gift itself. (Unlike many of today's preachers who are seeking a gift from their listeners.) But Paul says he was seeking the profit that increases to their account. The NASB Bible and some other Bible translations have taken the Greek word 'karpos' and translated it as 'profit'. However, every other time that this word is used in the New Testament it is translated as 'fruit'.

> 'But the fruit (KARPOS) of the Spirit is love, joy, peace, patience, kindness, goodness, faithfulness, 23 gentleness, self-control; against such things there is no law.'
> Galatians 5:22-23

> 'Beware of the false prophets, who come to you in sheep's clothing, but inwardly are ravenous wolves. 16 You will know them by their fruits (KARPOS). Grapes are not gathered from thorn bushes nor figs from thistles, are they?'
> Matthew 7:15-16

It is this fruit that we are told we will know false prophets by. It is this fruit that is seen in us through the Holy Spirit. Therefore, when Paul was talking to the Philippians about an increase in their account because of their giving, he was talking about an increase of fruit, or character. This aligns with other teachings about fruit in the New Testament.

The King James translation gets it right.

> 'Not because I desire a gift: but I desire fruit that may abound to your account.'

*Philippians 4:17*
*(King James Version)*

This also sheds new light on the next verses.

*'But I have received everything in full and have an abundance; I am amply supplied, having received from Epaphroditus what you have sent, a fragrant aroma, an acceptable sacrifice, well-pleasing to God. [19] And my God will supply all your needs according to His riches in glory in Christ Jesus.'*
*Philippians 4:18-19*

This is about supplying all our needs to bring about fruit, it is not about a provision for our greed or selfish desires. To sum up these verses in Philippians, it is not about us seeking gifts but seeking fruit.

## 7. Tithing, the financial giving of 10%

Once again, I encourage you to allow the Holy Spirit to be your teacher, study the Scripture, and see what it says as we deal with this controversial subject of tithing.

Tithing today is the practice of giving 10% your income. One of the main Scriptures used to teach the requirement for people to tithe is found in the Old Testament book of Malachi.

> 'Will a man rob God? Yet you are robbing Me! But you say, "How have we robbed You?" In tithes and offerings. $^9$ You are cursed with a curse, for you are robbing Me, the whole nation of you! $^{10}$ Bring the whole tithe into the storehouse, so that there may be food in My house, and test Me now in this,' says the Lord of hosts, 'if I will not open for you the windows of heaven and pour out for you a blessing until it overflows. $^{11}$ Then I will rebuke the devourer for you, so that it will not destroy the fruits of the ground; nor will your vine in the field cast its grapes,' says the Lord of hosts.'
> Malachi 3:8-11

I once worked in a position where my income would fluctuate every week. As a young Christian that believed in the necessity of tithing, I would carefully work out 10% of my income so that I could put it in the offering every Sunday. However, when I understood New Testament giving, I found myself giving far more than the obligated tithe. No longer did my income determine how much I gave; it was determined by the spirit, love and generosity.

While my intention of giving 10% was good, it was based on several wrong teachings. These included:

## Wrong teaching 1: Tithing is compulsory for Christians

This wrong teaching says that God requires all Christians to give 10% of all their income.

While tithing is biblical, it is mentioned and practised (albeit differently to today) in the Old Testament. The New Testament has only a few mentions of tithing such as in Luke 11:42, where Jesus criticised the Pharisees for tithing out of religious duty and wrong priorities.

> 'But woe to you Pharisees! You give a tenth of mint, rue, and every kind of herb, and you bypass justice and love for God. These things you should have done without neglecting the others.'
> Luke 11:42

> [10] "Two men went up into the temple to pray, one a Pharisee and the other a tax collector. [11] The Pharisee stood and was praying this to himself: 'God, I thank You that I am not like other people: swindlers, unjust,

*adulterers, or even like this tax collector. [12] I fast twice a week; I pay tithes of all that I get.' [13] But the tax collector, standing some distance away, was even unwilling to lift up his eyes to heaven, but was beating his breast, saying, 'God, be merciful to me, the sinner!' [14] I tell you, this man went to his house justified rather than the other; for everyone who exalts himself will be humbled, but he who humbles himself will be exalted."*
*Luke 18:10-14*

Where tithing is mentioned by Jesus in Luke 11:42 and Luke 18:11-12, it carries a negative connotation and a sense of mandated religious duty with mixed priorities. This is the opposite when Jesus speaks about caring for the needy by generous or sacrificial giving.

In the verses in Luke, Jesus does not condemn tithing, but rather the attitude and wrong priority. He tells the Pharisee that they should have done those things without neglecting the other things. The scripture is referring to the love and justice of God and their priorities were on tithing more than love and justice. Every example of giving we see in the New Testament is not an obligated tithe but rather generosity motivated by love, justice and compassion, directed towards those in need.

Like many other things that Jesus taught in the New Testament, he expected a response that went beyond the Old Testament. For example:

The Old Testament commands us not to commit

murder; Jesus said being angry with someone is as if you've already murdered them. (Matthew 5:21-22) The Old Testament condemns adultery; Jesus says if you even look at someone with lust it's as if you've already committed adultery with them. (Matthew 5:27-28)

And when it comes to giving:
The Old Testament has tithing and special offerings that were commanded and mandatory for some; where the New Testament teaches us to give generously, sacrificially, not forced or under compulsion, secretly and with the right attitude.

Some may argue that Jesus never abolished tithing, however, there is no command anywhere in the New Testament that speaks about giving just 10% of anything.
Jesus' example to us was sacrificial; He never just gave 10% of His life for us, He gave it all. In the New Testament, we are taught to give generously in all areas (not just financially). Jesus doesn't want us to follow him just 10% of the time, he wants 100% commitment from us.

Romans goes on to say it well:

> 'Therefore, brothers, by the mercies of God, I urge you to present your bodies as a living sacrifice, holy and pleasing to God; this is your spiritual worship.'
> Romans 12:1

A living sacrifice sounds like an oxymoron. To be living and a sacrifice seems contradictory, as such a living sacrifice is an oxymoron. While every Old Testament sacrificial offering was killed to become an offering, our bodies remain alive but should still be sacrificed for God's will. It is only in the New Testament that we are asked to present our bodies as living sacrifices.

In the New Testament, tithing is not compulsory for a Christian, however, as living sacrifices, generosity is expected from those who follow Christ. Generosity cannot be measured by a percentage, nor does it just include finances.

When Jesus addressed the Pharisees in Luke 11:42, he didn't condemn the giving of 10%. He said they should keep doing it but not neglect justice and love while doing it.

> 'But woe to you Pharisees! You give a tenth of mint, rue, and every kind of herb, and you bypass justice and love for God. These things you should have done without neglecting the others.'
> Luke 11:42

And in 1 John 3:16-17, love goes way beyond the giving of 10%.

> 'This is how we have come to know love: He laid down His life for us. We should also lay down our lives for our brothers. $^{17}$ If anyone has this world's goods and sees his brother in need but closes his eyes to his need

> — how can God's love reside in him?'
> 1 John 3:16-17

The Pharisees gave 10% but they missed the whole point. They simply gave out of religious duty and tradition. Love and justice would make us not give 10% out of duty, but rather sacrificially be prepared to lay down our lives for our brothers and to give to their needs.

If you are tithing because you believe you have to or you are compelled to; or if you are giving more than 10% out of obligation or compulsion, then I would recommend for you to pause your giving and check your motivation towards giving.
Check your attitude and when you give, follow the New Testament principles of giving generously and secretly to those in need.

**Wrong teaching 2: By not tithing you are cursed**
By not tithing you are cursed, by tithing God will divinely bless you with protection from the devourer. This is another wrong teaching that arrives from Malachi 3:8-11.

> '"Will a man rob God? Yet you are robbing Me! But you say, "How have we robbed You?" In tithes and offerings. ⁹ You are cursed with a curse, for you are robbing Me, the whole nation of you! ¹⁰ Bring the whole tithe into the storehouse, so that there may be food in My house, and test Me now in this," says the

> Lord of hosts, "if I will not open for you the windows of heaven and pour out for you a blessing until it overflows. [11] Then I will rebuke the devourer for you, so that it will not destroy the fruits of the ground; nor will your vine in the field cast its grapes," says the Lord of hosts.'
> Malachi 3:8-11

The idea that God would curse us for not financially giving to Him goes against His character. While He is a just God and as such needs to uphold justice, which involves judgement, His future judgement will be based on unrighteousness and unrepentant sin, and not on financial giving.

In the New Testament Jesus cursed the fig tree for not bearing fruit.

> 'Seeing a lone fig tree by the road, He came to it and found nothing on it except leaves only; and He said to it, "No longer shall there ever be any fruit from you." And at once the fig tree withered.'
> Matthew 21:19

Fruit in the New Testament is never about money and material provisions; it always represents character and more eternal lasting traits.

> 'But the fruit of the Spirit is love, joy, peace, patience, kindness, goodness, faithfulness, [23] gentleness, self-control; against such things there is no law.'
> Galatians 5:22-23

> *'You did not choose Me but I chose you, and appointed you that you would go and bear fruit, and that your fruit would remain, so that whatever you ask of the Father in My name He may give to you. [17] This I command you, that you love one another.'*
> John 15:16-17

The idea that God will curse us because of our lack of financial giving or tithing does not align with the New Testament principle of bearing fruit, nor does the idea that we are blessed more when we tithe. According to the New Testament, we have been blessed with every spiritual blessing.

> *'To the saints who are at Ephesus and who are faithful in Christ Jesus: [2] Grace to you and peace from God our Father and the Lord Jesus Christ.*
> *[3] Blessed be the God and Father of our Lord Jesus Christ, who has blessed us with every spiritual blessing in the heavenly places in Christ, [4] just as He chose us in Him before the foundation of the world, that we would be holy and blameless before Him.'*
> Ephesians 1:1-4

The blessing of Ephesian 1:3 is aimed at the faithful saints, those who are chosen to be holy and blameless. It is not based on their giving. The Pharisees gave and were not blessed because of it.

> *'But woe to you Pharisees! You give a tenth of mint, rue, and every kind of herb, and you bypass justice and love for God. These things you should have done without neglecting the others.'*
> Luke 11:42

In Matthew 23:13-35, we find eight warnings or eight woes addressed at the Pharisees, even though they tithed. The fact that they tithed did not command a blessing but instead attracted a warning on their religious attitude. God will not curse you if you don't tithe. He does, however, warn those that tithe out of a wrong motive. Today some people that tithe do so out of obligation or fear: obligation to a religious system and fear that they will be cursed for not tithing. Obligation and fear are never seen as good motives.

Fear does not come from God.

> *'For God has not given us a spirit of fearfulness, but one of power, love, and sound judgment.'*
> 2 Timothy 1:7

**Wrong teaching 3: The storehouse is the local church**
Some churches will use Malachi 3 to justify the requirement to tithe to your local church today. This wrong teaching arrives from Malachi 3:10, where they wrongly translate the word 'storehouse' to mean 'local church.'

> *'Bring the whole tithe into **the storehouse**, so that there may be food in **My house**.'*
> *Malachi 3:10*

This Scripture refers to two very distinct places, they were different but connected. There is 'the storehouse' and then there is 'God's house'. These places are two completely different words. Storehouse is also translated and used as 'treasury'. God's house or His Temple is never seen as a treasury but a place of glory, a place for prayer, a place of holiness.

> *'And He said to them, "It is written, My house will be called a house of prayer. But you are making it a den of thieves!"'*
> *Matthew 21:13*

In Malachi's day, there were storehouses where a tithe of fresh produce and flocks were brought to and stored. You can see these two distinct rooms in Chronicles where Hezekiah instructed chambers to be built to store the tithe.

> *'Hezekiah told them to prepare chambers in the Lord's temple, and they prepared them. ¹² The offering, the tenth, and the dedicated things were brought faithfully. Conaniah the Levite was the officer in charge of them, and his brother Shimei was second.'*
> *2 Chronicles 31:11-12*

The storehouse was a place that supplied provisions to the needy, the priests and the Levites. Even though the needs of the priests and Levites were met through the storehouse, this does not excuse today's church leaders (Pastor, Apostle, Evangelist or whatever title they use) to greedily expect believers to give to their personal needs.
Who is the New Testament priest?
Who is the New Testament Levite who is set aside for ministry to the Lord?
Is it not every believer and follower of Jesus Christ?

*'But you are A chosen race, A royal priesthood, A holy nation, A people for God's own possession, so that you may proclaim the excellencies of Him who has called you out of darkness into His marvelous light.'*
*1 Peter 2:9*

1 Peter 2:9 refers to all believers as priests. As such, we can justify the pattern of the New Testament church where the needs of all believers, widows, and orphans were met.

*'Now all the believers were together and held all things in common. [45] They sold their possessions and property and distributed the proceeds to all, as anyone had a need.'*
*Acts 2:44-45*

*'Pure and undefiled religion before our God and Father is this: to look after orphans and widows in their*

> *distress and to keep oneself unstained by the world.'*
> *James 1:27*

What would be the equivalent of the storehouse today? If we are to insist on tithing, then we need to know where our tithe should go.

Some churches would teach that the storehouse is the place in which you get fed, thus your local church, which is where you go every week for spiritual food. However, the Old Testament storehouse was a place that offered physical food and essentials to people as needed.

Today, most church buildings are not used as storage to distribute anything physical.

For a church to insist that the tithe goes to the local church or storehouse they need to ignore other Scripture showing that tithes can be paid elsewhere. Deuteronomy 14:23-27 is just one of them.

> *'You are to eat a tenth of your grain, new wine, and oil, and the firstborn of your herd and flock, in the presence of Yahweh your God at the place where He chooses to have His name dwell, so that you will always learn to fear the Lord your God. [24] But if the distance is too great for you to carry it, since the place where Yahweh your God chooses to put His name is too far away from you and since the Lord your God has blessed you, [25] then exchange it for money, take the money in your hand, and go to the place the Lord your*

> God chooses. ²⁶ You may spend the money on anything you want: cattle, sheep, wine, beer, or anything you desire. You are to feast there in the presence of the Lord your God and rejoice with your family. ²⁷ Do not neglect the Levite within your gates, since he has no portion or inheritance among you.'
> Deuteronomy 14:23-27
> (Holman Christian Standard Bible)

This Scripture tells us two things that we can and should do with our tithe that most churches will tell us not to do.
1. It tells us we are to eat our tithe at the place God has put His name on.
2. If we can't carry it or get it to a place that God has His name on, we are to change our tithe for money and spend the money on anything we want and then have a feast with God and our family, not neglecting others.

Nowhere in Scripture will we find the word storehouse being used to describe a place where we get spiritually fed or a place of worship or prayer. However, we do find references like the one we previously quoted in 2 Chronicles 31:11-12, where it refers to a place of welfare and practical provision. This too supports what the New Testament teaches; to give and offer practical welfare and provisions to those in need, to support our brothers, widows and orphans.

*'If anyone has this world's goods and sees his brother in need but closes his eyes to his need — how can God's love reside in him?'*
1 John 3:17

*'Religion that God our Father accepts as pure and faultless is this: to look after orphans and widows in their distress and to keep oneself from being polluted by the world.'*
James 1:27

*'But if anyone does not provide for his own, and especially for those of his household, he has denied the faith and is worse than an unbeliever.'*
1 Timothy 5:8

## 8. What Malachi says about tithing

As stated earlier, Malachi 3:10 is one of the main Scriptures that is misinterpreted to compel people to tithe.

> *"'Bring the whole tithe into the storehouse, so that there may be food in My house, and test Me now in this," says the Lord of hosts, "if I will not open for you the windows of heaven and pour out for you a blessing until it overflows."'*
> Malachi 3:10

Out of fear of robbing God some people are told to tithe. They are incorrectly taught that by tithing they keep God happy and He pours out his blessing on them; but when they don't, they arouse God's anger and He pronounces curses on them. Blessings or curses can then be determined by your financial giving. How odd it is that we often hear preached that God's blessings are free but on the other hand we need to give 10% of our income to obtain them. Is it similar to Simon the sorcerer in Acts 8 when he offered money to buy God's gift and blessing?

> *Now when Simon saw that the Spirit was bestowed through the laying on of the apostles' hands, he offered them money, [19] saying, "Give this authority to me as well, so that everyone on whom I lay my hands may receive the Holy Spirit." [20] But Peter said to him, "May your silver perish with you, because you thought you could obtain the gift of God with money! [21] You have no part or portion in this matter,*

*for your heart is not right before God.*
*Acts 8:18-21*

Let's have a closer look at the book of Malachi.

Malachi was a prophet in the days of Nehemiah, and most of his message and ministry was the calling out of judgment in a time that was full of corrupt priests and wicked practices. Many people in his days had a false sense of security in their privileged relationship with God.

As you study the entire book of Malachi, you quickly discover that it is addressing the corruption, wickedness and false security of the day. This corruption and wickedness could be seen in many areas, including how the tithes and offerings were being collected and distributed. There were rules and guidelines not only about how the tithe should be collected, but also about the purpose of the tithe and how it should be distributed.

The book of Deuteronomy lays a good foundation for the Old Testament tithe. It clearly explains that the Levites, foreigners, widows and orphans were entitled to the food brought into the storehouse from the tithe; this is why the tithe was received.

*'"When you have finished paying all the tithe of your increase in the third year, the year of tithing, then you shall give it to the Levite, to the stranger, to the*

orphan and to the widow, that they may eat in your towns and be satisfied. ¹³ You shall say before the Lord your God, 'I have removed the sacred portion from my house, and also have given it to the Levite and the alien, the orphan and the widow, according to all Your commandments which You have commanded me; I have not transgressed or forgotten any of Your commandments.'"
Deuteronomy 26:12-13

'At the end of every third year you shall bring out all the tithe of your produce in that year, and shall deposit it in your town. ²⁹ The Levite, because he has no portion or inheritance among you, and the alien, the orphan and the widow who are in your town, shall come and eat and be satisfied, in order that the Lord your God may bless you in all the work of your hand which you do.'
Deuteronomy 14:28-29

¹² "When you have finished paying all the tithe of your increase in the third year, the year of tithing, then you shall give it to the Levite, to the stranger, to the orphan and to the widow, that they may eat in your towns and be satisfied. ¹³ You shall say before the Lord your God, 'I have removed the sacred portion from my house, and also have given it to the Levite and the alien, the orphan and the widow, according to all Your commandments which You have commanded me; I have not transgressed or forgotten any of Your

*commandments.*
*Deuteronomy 26:12-13*

The tithe was to supply for the needs of the widows, orphans, foreigners and Levitical priests. The Levitical priest received a portion of the tithe for their support because they had no inheritance in Canaan and they did not own land or property. As such, they were entitled to receive support from the storehouse along with the foreigners, widows and orphans.

The book of Malachi is a book of woes and judgements directed at God's people. In Malachi 3:5 we see judgement pronounced on those who are with withholding wages, neglecting widows and orphans, and turning away aliens and foreigners. All of these were meant to be provided for from the tithe that was brought to the storehouse.

> *'"Then I will draw near to you for judgment; and I will be a swift witness against the sorcerers and against the adulterers and against those who swear falsely, and against those who oppress the wage earner in his wages, the widow and the orphan, and those who turn aside the alien and do not fear Me," says the Lord of hosts.'*
> *Malachi 3:5*

Malachi 3:5 is directly before the famous tithing verse

and as such forms the foundation, the launching pad to it.

> 'For I, the Lord, do not change; therefore you, O sons of Jacob, are not consumed.
> [7] "From the days of your fathers you have turned aside from My statutes and have not kept them. Return to Me, and I will return to you," says the Lord of hosts. "But you say, 'How shall we return?'
> You Have Robbed God
> [8] "Will a man rob God? Yet you are robbing Me! But you say, 'How have we robbed You?' In tithes and offerings. [9] You are cursed with a curse, for you are robbing Me, the whole nation of you! [10] Bring the whole tithe into the storehouse, so that there may be food in My house, and test Me now in this," says the Lord of hosts, "if I will not open for you the windows of heaven and pour out for you a blessing until it overflows."'
> Malachi 3:6-10

Clearly, the tithe was a way to provide for the needs of the Levites, the foreigners, the widows and the orphans. Malachi 3:6-10 is a warning about the abuse and misuse of the tithe as it was not being distributed to those in need, and as such God was being robbed.

We find in the book of Proverbs that God is mocked and insulted by someone that oppresses the poor.

> *He who oppresses the poor reproaches, mocks, and insults his Maker,*
> *but he who is kind and merciful to the needy honors Him*
> *Proverbs 14:31*
> *(Amplified version)*

The original Hebrew word that is translated as "oppresses" in Proverbs 14:31, is "ashaq" and is the same word used in Malachi 3:5, which links the oppressing of the poor to the robbing God in Malachi 3:8.

> *'"Then I will draw near to you for judgment; and I will be a swift witness against the sorcerers and against the adulterers and against those who swear falsely, and against those who <u>oppress</u> the wage earner in his wages, the widow and the orphan, and those who turn aside the alien and do not fear Me," says the Lord of hosts.'*
> *Malachi 3:5*

**God is robbed when the poor are oppressed.**
While some preachers may use Malachi 3 to express a warning about robbing God if you do not tithe, the warning applies to the unjust distribution of the tithe. Preachers who fatten up their own nest, who renovate and build bigger buildings, all from the tithe of the people, are robbing God because they are not distributing the whole tithe to the needy.

*Son of man, prophesy against the shepherds of Israel, prophesy and say to them, 'Thus says the Lord God to the shepherds: "Woe to the shepherds of Israel who feed themselves! Should not the shepherds feed the flocks? ³ You eat the fat and clothe yourselves with the wool; you slaughter the fatlings, but you do not feed the flock. ⁴ The weak you have not strengthened, nor have you healed those who were sick, nor bound up the broken, nor brought back what was driven away, nor sought what was lost; but with force and cruelty you have ruled them.*
*Ezekiel 34:2-4*
*(NKJV)*

The shepherds need to trust God that there will be enough food in the storehouse when they distribute it to the needy first. Much like when Jesus fed the 5000, the five loaves and two fish were distributed firstly to the people, and then God provided an abundance of leftovers for the disciples. If the disciples had fed themselves first and consumed the loaves and fish, would have they missed the miraculous provision? Would have the food ran out, producing no leftovers?

From my close examination of Scripture, it appears that the warning in Malachi 3 about robbing God is not about the receiving of the tithe, but rather the distribution of it.

If preachers insist that their congregation practices the Old Testament principle of tithing, then their congregation should also be able to expect that the tithe is distributed biblically amongst the needy.

## 9. The Melchizedek argument

To understand this chapter, we need to briefly examine what is called by some "ceremonial law". Ceremonial laws are Old Testament precepts that deal with worshipping God, ritual cleansings and judicial precepts. There are many of these listed throughout the Old Testament, predominately in the books of Exodus, Leviticus, Numbers and Deuteronomy.

Ceremonial Law includes:
- Instructions on pleasing and regaining right standing with God through animal sacrifices and other cleansing ceremonies.
- Festivals and feasts that remember God's work in Israel.
- Dietary and clothing restrictions designed to distinguish Israelites from their pagan neighbours.
- Signs that point to the coming Messiah such as the Sabbath, circumcision, Passover, and the redemption of the firstborn.

The New Testament church is not just the nation of Israel; Jesus death and resurrection opened it up for all. Therefore, New Testament Christians are not bound by Old Testament ceremonial laws. Since the church is not the nation of Israel, memorial festivals such as the Feast of Weeks and Passover do not apply.

With the death of Jesus, all Old Testament ceremonial laws ceased, never to be used again to condemn us. Therefore, there are no New Testament examples of Christians tithing, just as we no longer sacrifice goats and bulls to cover our sins.

> *When you were dead in your transgressions and the uncircumcision of your flesh, He made you alive together with Him, having forgiven us all our transgressions, [14] having cancelled out the certificate of debt consisting of decrees against us, which was hostile to us; and He has taken it out of the way, having nailed it to the cross. [15] When He had disarmed the rulers and authorities, He made a public display of them, having triumphed over them through Him. [16] Therefore no one is to act as your judge in regard to food or drink or in respect to a festival or a new moon or a Sabbath day— [17] things which are a mere shadow of what is to come; but the substance belongs to Christ.*
> *Colossians 2:13-17*

The Melchizedek argument teaches that tithing was not part of the ceremonial codes as it happened before any law was introduced when Abram tithed to Melchizedek. This is wrong teaching.

> *'Then Melchizedek, king of Salem, brought out bread and wine; he was a priest to God Most High. [19] He blessed him and said:*

> *"Abram is blessed by God Most High,*
> *Creator of heaven and earth,*
> *[20] and I give praise to God Most High*
> *who has handed over your enemies to you."*
> *And Abram gave him a tenth of everything.'*
> *Genesis 14:18-20*

To claim that tithing was set in place before the law and thus continues to be a requirement today is wrong.
Consider the following:
- When you read this whole Scripture in context, you discover that when Abram tithed to Melchizedek, he tithed from the spoils of war and not from his general income.
- This was a once-off activity and not a regular weekly event.
- There were also many other customs like animal sacrifices and circumcision, all of which were introduced before Moses and are no longer practised today.

In Numbers 31, Israel was asked to give 1/500th and 1/50th of the spoils of war. This is significantly less than what Abram gave to Melchizedek, showing that the tithe of Abram was not a lasting or standing ordinance.

> [28] *'"Set aside a tribute for the Lord from what belongs to the fighting men who went out to war: one out of*

*every 500 humans, cattle, donkeys, sheep, and goats.* ²⁹ *Take the tribute from their half and give it to Eleazar the priest as a contribution to the Lord.* ³⁰ *From the Israelites' half, take one out of every 50 from the people, cattle, donkeys, sheep, and goats, all the livestock, and give them to the Levites who perform the duties of the Lord's tabernacle."'*
*Numbers 31:28-30*


To use what happened with Abram and Melchizedek as a reason why we must tithe today, is just a wrong teaching to motivate and beg us to give. It results in us giving to meet a legal requirement and establishing a respectable relationship, rather than giving generously out of love and compassion.

## 10. Summarizing tithing

With tithing being such a big topic and taking up a large portion of this book, I have included this short chapter to summarize some basic points about tithing. Scripture for these points have been discussed in the last few chapters.

- Old Testament tithing was not required every week.
- There is no evidence that tithing was practised by New Testament Christians.
- Tithing was a way to supply the material needs of the Levites (that could not own land), widows, orphans and foreigners.
- God's blessing does <u>NOT</u> depend on tithing.
- Old Testament tithing was based on produce and livestock, not money (yes, money did exist in the Old Testament).
- The Old Testament storehouse is not the same as the local church.

**Recommendations for people that choose to tithe**
While tithing is not compulsory, some people may choose to tithe. Deciding to give 10% of your income is not a bad thing to do, but then giving any amount is not a bad thing. It all depends on your attitude and motivation – why are you giving?
When you choose to give or tithe, remember to follow biblical principles:
- Don't tithe out of duty.
- Give because you want to, not because someone

told you that you have to.
- Give generously and do not allow anyone, except God tell you how much you should give.
- Give your gift or tithe to where God directs you. You are not obliged to give it to your local church.
- Give secretly and do not expect a financial reward.

**Beware of any teaching or ministry that twists Scripture to get you to financially give to them.**
As I said earlier, I choose not to give to any ministry that twists Scripture to compel me to give to them. I prefer to practice the biblical principles and give anonymously and directly to the recipient.

## 11. Turning over the money changers' tables

> 'Then they came to Jerusalem. And He entered the temple and began to drive out those who were buying and selling in the temple, and overturned the tables of the money changers and the seats of those who were selling doves; [16] and He would not permit anyone to carry merchandise through the temple. [17] And He began to teach and say to them, "Is it not written, 'MY house shall be called A house of prayer for all the nations'? But you have made it a robbers' den."'
> Mark 11:15-17

Some may say this well-known account of Jesus cleansing the temple was a once-off cultural occurrence that was caused by sinful people using the temple to make an unethical profit. However, in it there are warnings for us about how the institutionalised church and we individually, handle money and conduct money-making business.

1. Warnings for our individual conduct
Biblically, our bodies are His temple.

> 'Do you not know that you are a temple of God and that the Spirit of God dwells in you?'
> 1 Corinthians 3:16

There is a warning for each of us individually with regards to trading, being ethical and how we handle money.

What is the focus of our temple? Have we turned it into a den of robbers? Maybe we too need to repent and refocus.

## 2. Warnings for the institutionalised church

Jesus went into a physical place called a temple, it was a building, a place that was known as the temple. In this place, He turned over the money changers' tables.

Whether we consider our bodies or a physical building as His temple, we need to adhere to the warning given to us in these verses.
For the sake of understanding, this chapter will explain some of those warnings as they apply to the traditional understanding of 'church'; that being a building where Christians gather normally on a Sunday. However, similar warnings can apply to us personally.

In the book of The Revelation, we read God's letters to seven churches and while these churches were all judged by their deeds, the church of Laodicea was also judged on their attitude and focus on money and material possessions.

> 'Because you say, "I am rich, and have become wealthy, and have need of nothing," and you do not know that you are wretched and miserable and poor and blind and naked, [18] I advise you to buy from Me gold refined by fire so that you may become rich, and white garments so that you may clothe yourself, and

> *that the shame of your nakedness will not be revealed; and eye salve to anoint your eyes so that you may see.* <sup>19</sup> *Those whom I love, I reprove and discipline; therefore be zealous and repent.'*
> Revelation 3:17-19

It would appear that Laodicea and the temple in Jesus's days had a focus on material wealth that drew them away from the main focus of God.
This has been a common problem throughout history.

In 1517 Martin Luther wrote his Ninety-five Theses, which addressed the practices of the Catholic church selling indulgences. People were told they could buy an indulgence and get their deceased loved one a reduced sentence in purgatory.
Was this any different to what was happening when Jesus cleansed the temple?

With some of the current practices within churches and ministries, are we focused more on money than prayer?

> *'For the love of money is a root of all kinds of evil, and by craving it, some have wandered away from the faith and pierced themselves with many pains.'*
> 1 Timothy 6:10

Have you ever heard a televangelist promise a tenfold return on your gift, or your prayers being answered if you send him money, or purchase his holy item?

What about a preacher that promises you healing or blessing if you simply sow a big financial seed? Is this the equivalent to the financial practices that were happening when Jesus cleansed the temple?

To understand this further and to answer our aforementioned questions, let us examine Scripture.

> [12] 'And Jesus entered the temple and drove out all those who were buying and selling in the temple, and overturned the tables of the money changers and the seats of those who were selling doves. [13] And He said to them, "It is written, 'MY house shall be called A house of prayer'; but you are making it a robbers' den."'
> Matthew 21:12-13

> 'Jesus entered the temple and began to drive out those who were selling, [46] saying to them, "It is written, 'And MY house shall be A house of prayer,' but you have made it a robbers' den."'
> Luke 19:45-46

Matthew 21:12 tells us that Jesus drove out of the temple those that were buying and selling, exchanging money and selling doves. It is interesting that the exchanging of money and selling of doves is specifically mentioned in addition to just buying and selling. It is commonly believed that people were being compelled to exchange their money for the acceptable offering currency and to buy approved animals for sacrifice.

It was about greed and the turning of the temple from a holy sanctuary and refuge to a place where the greedy could feed their greed and the poor would be compelled to part with their money, to fulfil their religious duties.

When Jesus addressed it, he said:
'It is written, "MY house shall be called A house of prayer"; but you are making it a robbers' den.'

We find this written in two Old Testament verses. House of prayer derives from:

> '"Even those I will bring to My holy mountain
> And make them joyful in My house of prayer.
> Their burnt offerings and their sacrifices will be acceptable on My altar;
> For My house will be called a house of prayer for all the peoples."'
> Isaiah 56:7

Isaiah 56:7 in context is talking about foreigners being welcome in the temple and how the offerings and sacrifices they brought would be accepted by the Lord. There was no need for them to purchase a different animal or exchange their coins.

Den of robbers derives from:

> '"Has this house, which is called by My name, become a den of robbers in your sight? Behold, I, even I, have

> *seen it," declares the Lord.'*
> *Jeremiah 7:11*

Jeremiah 7 is calling the people of Judah to repentance because of their unrighteous ways, their deceitful words, their oppression and the burdens that they put on the foreigners, widows and orphans. In the Temple, similar oppression and burdens were being put on the people, as such Jesus declared that they had turned the temple into a den of robbers.

In light of these Scriptures that Jesus quoted from, we would need to admit that there are practices happening today within the church that has turned it into a den of robbers.

The church of Laodicea (Revelation 3:14-22) was deceived by what they saw as wealth and success, yet they were wretched, miserable, poor, blind and naked because their perceived wealth was not defined by Jesus, but by the world. As a result, they were called to repentance and told to put on eye salve so that they could see. Their love for material wealth had taken away their focus and the purpose for which God had called them. They were no longer the house of prayer, of refuge and worship, but a place for material profit and prosperity.

Unfortunately, it sounds very familiar to what is happening in some churches today.
While legitimate fundraising activities may be needed

to maintain the institutionalised church, the promotion of those activities within the church may cause our focus to change and become that of a business. Our focus may change from God and faith in His provision, to money, wealth and material prosperity.

Another thing Jesus did when He turned over the money changers' tables was that He did not permit anyone to carry merchandise through the temple.

> *'and He would not permit anyone to carry merchandise through the temple.'*
> Mark 11:16

He was so sickened by what He saw happening at the temple that even to carry merchandise through offended Him. Yet today, we justify the selling of merchandise, coffee, meals and more not only in the church, but throughout the church service as well. Some may justify it as necessary but maybe it is more of a problem with today's church model. This we will discuss in the next chapter.

## 12. The business of the church

I have heard some preachers explain the problem Jesus had with the temple was that fees were required to worship, or that the people trading were dishonest in their trades and for those reasons Jesus was justified in driving them out. Often this argument is used to excuse churches or ministries from an over-emphasis on money, fundraising and trading merchandise.

The NASB translation of the Bible uses the word 'business' to explain what they were doing.

> *"Take these things away; stop making My Father's house a place of business."*
> John 2:16

This presents a modern-day church problem as most churches are set up as a business.

In our modern world, for an organisation to own a building, equipment, to have a bank account, etc., it needs to be recognised by the government as a legal entity. Any organisation that does not have legal government recognition cannot legally own anything (building, equipment, etc.) and cannot have bank accounts. As such, most modern churches have become legal entities, either individually or through a movement or denomination.

To be a legal entity requires the organisation to operate under specific rules and instructions.

It is similar to a business; which needs to register with the government, have its bank account and follow government rules and reporting.
The problem is that for a recognised organisation or business to survive it needs to make a financial profit. It is a legal entity, and just like us it needs money to pay its bills.

When the church becomes a legal entity, it becomes an institution, incorporation or organisation and it is subject to governmental rules and reporting.
Therefore, it needs financial stability to survive.

Every business needs to trade and have customers. For the church, its members become its customers and its most regular source of income becomes the tithe of its customers. Every business needs a funding source. This is one reason why many churches compel their adherents to tithe, as the funds are needed to pay bills like building expenses, wages, insurances, utilities and other day-to-day running costs.

In John 2:16, when Jesus said, 'Take these things away; stop making My Father's house a place of business', the word he used for 'business' was the Greek word 'emporion', which in its most basic concept means 'a trading place'.

What determines a trading place? Is it not a place where a trade is made? There's trade in entertainment and sporting venues, you trade money for entertainment; there's trade in retail, you trade money for a product; there's trade with service providers, you trade money for service; and the list could go on.

Now, even though the church service is not meant to be about receiving, many people attend to receive something. Whether that be an emotional feeling from the music or a word from the Lord through the preacher, a trade is often made. Now, we can receive from the church service without trading as we don't need to give anything, albeit we feel less blessed and guilty for not giving when being compelled to give.

**The problem is not the receiving but the obligated trading to receive.**

The trading of the institutionalised church may include a trade of money for God's blessing; money for a miracle; money for more money. And let us not forget the trading that happens at the church café; merchandise store; etc.
It is common a practice for modern-day churches and preachers to be conducting business as part of the normal service of the gathering of believers, from receiving the tithes and offerings, to selling their books, coffee and lunch. We may excuse this as a necessary need, or you may just write me off as an extremist, but where is the example of faith of just trusting God to provide?

> 'Do not worry then, saying, "What will we eat?" or "What will we drink?" or "What will we wear for clothing?" ³² For the Gentiles eagerly seek all these things; for your heavenly Father knows that you need all these things.
> **³³ But seek first His kingdom and His righteousness, and all these things will be added to you.'**
> Matthew 6:31-33

The church that Jesus built was never intended to be a place of trading, it was never intended to be a place where you give something to get something. **The giving-to-get attitude is exactly what trade is.** In the Old Testament people gave their offering to receive forgiveness and blessing, but it is not so in the New Testament. The New Testament is a new covenant between God and man. It is about a free gift of salvation through the death and resurrection of Jesus Christ. You cannot purchase this; it simply requires faith with repentance.

> 'For by one offering He has perfected for all time those who are sanctified.'
> Hebrews 10:14

The giving-to-get attitude is reflected right throughout our world, culture and the institutionalised church. The giving-to-get attitude is almost the complete opposite of an attitude of surrender. To surrender something is to sacrifice it, to give it up without expecting any return. That is the big difference between trading and surrendering.

We have been taught to trade in our lives for Jesus' blessings and new life. For example, we are told to invite Jesus into our lives and He will bless us and give us a better life worth living. However, Jesus taught us to surrender our lives, to die to ourselves and our desires and follow Him.

> 'Then Jesus said to His disciples, "If anyone wishes to come after Me, he must deny himself, and take up his cross and follow Me. [25] For whoever wishes to save his life will lose it; but whoever loses his life for My sake will find it."'
> Matthew 16:24-25

Back to the business of the church. Whether we like it or not, when a church becomes a legal entity it needs to conduct business of some form. Some may argue here that the church being a legal entity, it is just the way it needs to be; it's just the laws of the land that we need to obey to operate a church.
But, is there a way the church could operate without trading or setting itself up as a legal entity or business? I believe so, but it takes faith and obedience to God's word and promises. He promises to provide for all our needs.

> 'Look at the birds of the air, that they do not sow, nor reap nor gather into barns, and yet your heavenly

> Father feeds them. Are you not worth much more than they? ²⁷ And who of you by being worried can add a single hour to his life? ²⁸ And why are you worried about clothing? Observe how the lilies of the field grow; they do not toil nor do they spin, ²⁹ yet I say to you that not even Solomon in all his glory clothed himself like one of these. ³⁰ But if God so clothes the grass of the field, which is alive today and tomorrow is thrown into the furnace, will He not much more clothe you? You of little faith! ³¹ Do not worry then, saying, "What will we eat?" or "What will we drink?" or "What will we wear for clothing?" ³² For the Gentiles eagerly seek all these things; for your heavenly Father knows that you need all these things. ³³ But seek first His kingdom and His righteousness, and all these things will be added to you.'
> Matthew 6:26-33

When a church is an institution, then it needs money to survive; it needs to pay rent, mortgage, bills, wages, insurance, etc. But God promises to provide and will provide for that which He has endorsed. If our focus is on the business to make money, then our focus has changed from that which it should be: Jesus.

> 'No one can serve two masters; for either he will hate the one and love the other, or he will be devoted to one and despise the other. You cannot serve God and wealth.'
> Matthew 6:24

The alternative to the church being a legal entity is for it to be how Jesus intended. Jesus didn't build a business, He built a community, a family. Jesus never ran a legally incorporated business. Yet Jesus said:

> '*I will build My church; and the gates of Hades will not overpower it.*'
> Matthew 16:18

It is often correctly said that the church is not a building, rather it is the people. Throughout the New Testament referencesto 'church', refer to 'the Ekklesia': a gathering of called out people, of Jesus' followers. This seems to be what is important to Jesus and the New Testament church; the gathering of the called-out ones. This gathering can gather without a legal entity, without a building, without insurance; just like we would gather with our friends at a park, at a barbecue, at a house, at a café. It can and should become like a gathering of your family, where no offering is needed to be collected, coffee is free and meals are freely shared.

In the truest sense, Ekklesia implies breaking away from the current secular and political system. The New Testament Ekklesia was called out of the Roman and Judean system. They came together and formed a new community where they had no other king but Jesus. No man ruled them, only Jesus. Is it any wonder that they ran into problems with the kings, rulers and hierarchy of the secular community?

There is a lot of good teaching available about the Ekklesia; the simple organic church, so I will not spend any more time on it in this book. Getting a good understanding of the Ekklesia, the church of the New Testament, will help us to focus less on money and more on God and the people for which He died for.

## 13. Who to give to?

Many of our churches today use a large proportion of their finances to purchase and build buildings; to purchase and update sound, video, lighting equipment; and to pay wages for their Pastors and other staff. While they may give a portion to assist the poor and needy, it is normally a very small portion of what is left after all the other expenses are paid.
These financial priorities seem to be out of line with the Bible.

While it is true that in the Old Testament they gave to help build God's temple (an actual physical building), there is not one New Testament example of giving to help purchase or build.

In the New Testament, God's people are His temple, and they gave to help and assist the needy.
In this chapter, we will look at many New Testament Scriptures and see what they say about who we should be giving to.

As stated earlier, the Old Testament tithe was set in place to provide for the needs of the Levites, widows, orphans and foreigners. The New Testament church didn't tithe but gave generously. Sometimes they even gave everything with the same purpose of the Old Testament tithe; to help meet the needs of those in need.

## 1. Giving to help our brothers

According to these scriptures, when we give to help others in need we demonstrate God's love.

*We know love by this, that He laid down His life for us; and we ought to lay down our lives for the brethren. [17] But whoever has the world's goods, and sees his brother in need and closes his heart against him, how does the love of God abide in him? [18] Little children, let us not love with word or with tongue, but in deed and truth.*
*1 John 3:16-18*

*'But if anyone does not provide for his own, and especially for those of his household, he has denied the faith and is worse than an unbeliever.*
*1 Timothy 5:8*

## 2. Giving to the needy

Giving to the needy is giving to God. Similar to Malachi 3:5-8 where the robbing of widows and orphans is the same as robbing God, so too in the New Testament parable of the sheep and goats, we see that giving or not giving to those in need is comparable to giving or not giving to Christ. It is a determining factor in our judgement of our eternal destination.

*'When the Son of Man comes in His glory, and all the angels with Him, then He will sit on the throne of His*

glory. ³² All the nations will be gathered before Him, and He will separate them one from another, just as a shepherd separates the sheep from the goats. ³³ He will put the sheep on His right and the goats on the left. ³⁴ Then the King will say to those on His right, "Come, you who are blessed by My Father, inherit the kingdom prepared for you from the foundation of the world.

³⁵ For I was hungry
and you gave Me something to eat;
I was thirsty
and you gave Me something to drink;
I was a stranger and you took Me in;
³⁶ I was naked and you clothed Me;
I was sick and you took care of Me;
I was in prison and you visited Me."

³⁷ Then the righteous will answer Him, "Lord, when did we see You hungry and feed You, or thirsty and give You something to drink? ³⁸ When did we see You a stranger and take You in, or without clothes and clothe You? ³⁹ When did we see You sick, or in prison, and visit You?"

⁴⁰ And the King will answer them, "I assure you: Whatever you did for one of the least of these brothers of Mine, you did for Me." ⁴¹ Then He will also say to those on the left, "Depart from Me, you who are cursed, into the eternal fire prepared for the Devil and his angels!

⁴² For I was hungry
and you gave Me nothing to eat;

> I was thirsty
> and you gave Me nothing to drink;
> ⁴³ I was a stranger
> and you didn't take Me in;
> I was naked
> and you didn't clothe Me,
> sick and in prison
> and you didn't take care of Me."
> ⁴⁴ Then they too will answer, "Lord, when did we see You hungry, or thirsty, or a stranger, or without clothes, or sick, or in prison, and not help You?"
> ⁴⁵ Then He will answer them, "I assure you: Whatever you did not do for one of the least of these, you did not do for Me either."
> ⁴⁶ And they will go away into eternal punishment, but the righteous into eternal life.'
> Matthew 25:31-46

James tells us that pure and undefiled religion will look after orphans and widows and keep oneself unstained by the world.

> 'Pure and undefiled religion before our God and Father is this: to look after orphans and widows in their distress and to keep oneself unstained by the world.'
> James 1:27

## 3. Giving to take care of each other

Throughout the New Testament, we find that giving to take care of others was commanded and expected. In Acts, they sold their possessions to ensure that everyone was looked after.

> *'And all those who had believed were together and had all things in common; $^{45}$ and they began selling their property and possessions and were sharing them with all, as anyone might have need.'*
> Acts 2:44-45

> *'And the congregation of those who believed were of one heart and soul; and not one of them claimed that anything belonging to him was his own, but all things were common property to them.'*
> Acts 4:32

> *'You yourselves know that these hands ministered to my own needs and to the men who were with me. $^{35}$ In everything I showed you that by working hard in this manner you must help the weak and remember the words of the Lord Jesus, that He Himself said, "It is more blessed to give than to receive."'*
> Acts 20:34-35

## 4. Giving to bring practical relief to others

In Corinthians, Paul gives some detailed instructions about a collection or offering they were receiving to bring practical relief to other people in another location.

> 'NOW CONCERNING the money contributed for [the relief of] the saints (God's people): you are to do the same as I directed the churches of Galatia to do. ² On the first [day] of each week, let each one of you [personally] put aside something and save it up as he has prospered [in proportion to what he is given], so that no collections will need to be taken after I come. ³ And when I arrive, I will send on those whom you approve and authorize with credentials to carry your gift [of charity] to Jerusalem.'
> 1 Corinthians 16:1-3 (AMP)

Note that in all the New Testament Scriptures there is never any mention of giving to a building, an institution, or a wealthy preacher. Nor was there ever a mention of sowing into a ministry to get a return. Giving in the New Testament was always directed toward those in need.

## 14. Exposing the prosperity doctrine

For years I have heard about a so-called 'prosperity doctrine', 'prosperity gospel', or the 'health and wealth gospel', and while identifying it may seem easy, it proved to be a lot more difficult than what I thought. I am still yet to find one preacher that admits to currently preaching a prosperity doctrine. Some may admit to preaching prosperity, but will justify it as being balanced with Scripture, using Scriptures about God's blessings and His abundance to back up their view of prosperity.

> 'Beloved, I pray that in all respects you may prosper and be in good health, just as your soul prospers.'
> 3 John 1:2

> 'The thief comes only to steal and kill and destroy; I came that they may have life, and have it abundantly.'
> John 10:10

These are just two of the Scriptures that I have heard used to justify the preaching of prosperity.

**The Bible does tell us that prosperity is God's desire for us, but God's measure of prosperity is not gold, silver or materialistic things. We need to get a Godly view of what prosperity is.**

When Jesus was tempted by satan, he was offered all the kingdoms of the world and their glory. This would give Him financial security and the material provisions that He would need to have a successful, prosperous ministry.

> *'Again, the devil took Him to a very high mountain and showed Him all the kingdoms of the world and their glory; ⁹ and he said to Him, "All these things I will give You, if You fall down and worship me."'* Matthew 4:8-9

I wonder how many preachers would take up satan's offer or have compromised for power, provisions, and financial security?

Another opportunity for Jesus to secure financial prosperity was when He called the fishermen.

> *⁴ 'When He had finished speaking, He said to Simon, "Put out into the deep water and let down your nets for a catch." ⁵ Simon answered and said, "Master, we worked hard all night and caught nothing, but I will do as You say and let down the nets." ⁶ When they had done this, they enclosed a great quantity of fish, and their nets began to break; ⁷ so they signaled to their partners in the other boat for them to come and help them. And they came and filled both of the boats, so that they began to sink.'*
> Luke 5:4-7

This would have been the biggest catch of fish that Simon Peter had ever had. It could bring financial security to him and help Jesus as He starts a ministry. However, Simon Peter and Jesus did not focus on the fish, the boats, or the finances that they could bring in. The Scripture says that they left everything behind to follow Him.

> ⁸ 'But when Simon Peter saw that, he fell down at Jesus' feet, saying, "Go away from me Lord, for I am a sinful man!" ⁹ For amazement had seized him and all his companions because of the catch of fish which they had taken; ¹⁰ and so also were James and John, sons of Zebedee, who were partners with Simon. And Jesus said to Simon, "Do not fear, from now on you will be catching men." ¹¹ When they had brought their boats to land, they left everything and followed Him.'
> Luke 5:8-11

The rich young ruler also presented another time for Jesus to be able to be financially prosperous.

> 'When Jesus heard this, He said to him, "One thing you still lack; sell all that you possess and distribute it to the poor, and you shall have treasure in heaven; and come, follow Me." ²³ But when he had heard these things, he became very sad, for he was extremely rich. ²⁴ And Jesus looked at him and said, "How hard it is for those who are wealthy to enter the kingdom of God!"'
> Luke 18:22-24

Jesus could've used this opportunity to try to convince the rich young ruler to give to His ministry, by selling all his possessions and sowing a seed into Jesus's ministry. But instead, Jesus told him to distribute it to the poor.

The true measure of prosperity is not wealth or material possessions; this is how the world measures prosperity, but it is not how God does it. The biblical word for 'prosper' means to thrive and be successful. Was Jesus' mission on earth successful? Of course it was, it achieved its purpose of reconciling man to God.

**Godly success is a true measure of biblical prosperity, not wealth and materialism.**

The pursuit of wealth and materialism is warned against in the Bible. Look at the following Scriptures:

> 'But those who want to get rich fall into temptation and a snare and many foolish and harmful desires which plunge men into ruin and destruction. $^{10}$ For the love of money is a root of all sorts of evil, and some by longing for it have wandered away from the faith and pierced themselves with many griefs. $^{11}$ But flee from these things, you man of God, and pursue righteousness, godliness, faith, love, perseverance and gentleness.'
> 1 Timothy 6:9-11

> 'Then He said to them, "Beware, and be on your guard against every form of greed; for not even when one has an abundance does his life consist of his possessions."'
> Luke 12:15

> 'But seek His kingdom, and these things will be added to you. $^{32}$ Do not be afraid, little flock, for your Father has chosen gladly to give you the kingdom.
> $^{33}$ Sell your possessions and give to charity; make yourselves

*money belts which do not wear out, an unfailing treasure in heaven, where no thief comes near nor moth destroys. ³⁴ For where your treasure is, there your heart will be also.'*
Luke 12:31-34

*'"No servant can serve two masters; for either he will hate the one and love the other, or else he will be devoted to one and despise the other. You cannot serve God and wealth." ¹⁴ Now the Pharisees, who were lovers of money, were listening to all these things and were scoffing at Him. ¹⁵ And He said to them, "You are those who justify yourselves in the sight of men, but God knows your hearts; for that which is highly esteemed among men is detestable in the sight of God."'*
Luke 16:13-15

*'Instruct those who are rich in this present world not to be conceited or to fix their hope on the uncertainty of riches, but on God, who richly supplies us with all things to enjoy. ¹⁸ Instruct them to do good, to be rich in good works, to be generous and ready to share, ¹⁹ storing up for themselves the treasure of a good foundation for the future, so that they may take hold of that which is life indeed.'*
1 Timothy 6:17-19

*Yes, they are greedy dogs*
*Which never have enough.*
*And they are shepherds*
*Who cannot understand;*
*They all look to their own way,*
*Every one for his own gain,*
*From his own territory.*
Isaiah 56:11

True biblical prosperity is to thrive and be successful, this is indeed what God wants for us. The Godly measure of success is not an abundance of money and material possessions, otherwise, someone that gains the whole world but forfeits their soul would still be very successful.

> *'For what will it profit a man if he gains the whole world and forfeits his soul? Or what will a man give in exchange for his soul?'*
> Matthew 16:26

> *'But godliness actually is a means of great gain when accompanied by contentment. ⁷ For we have brought nothing into the world, so we cannot take anything out of it either. ⁸ If we have food and covering, with these we shall be content.'*
> 1 Timothy 6:6-8

When we refer to the prosperity gospel today, it is a false gospel that is focussed upon money and material possessions but will justify its false teaching with Christ and His blessings towards us.

The foundation of the prosperity gospel is that God will bless you with more money and possessions. There is always more for you, it is not enough to be content with what you have. This contradicts 1 Timothy 6:6.

*'But godliness actually is a means of great gain when accompanied by contentment.'*
1 Timothy 6:6

Within the prosperity doctrine there is an underlining message that there are always more material items for you: more money, more property, a better car, etc. There never seems to be contentment with what you have, yet contentment is a common teaching throughout the New Testament.

**How to identify the prosperity gospel**
The following are some common traits of many prosperity preachers:

- A common theme in many of their messages is God's desire to bless everyone. While occasionally they may touch on other subjects, the foundation that God desires you to have material items and money underlines their message.

- They hardly ever mention the need for self-denial, taking up our crosses, or dying to the flesh (Luke 9:23; Matthew 10:38, 16:24), which Jesus commands us to do.

- Positive thinking about our personal situation is often equated with faith and is presented as a way by which one can obtain financial blessings.

- When receiving an offering, they share a message that compels (in fact, begs) you to give, with a promise of a materialistic return on what you give.

- There is often absence of any teaching about the necessity to suffer in the life of a believer. (2 Timothy 3:12;

Romans 8:17; Philippians 1:29).

- The personal wealth of the pastor is often far above the average lifestyle of his congregation. There is a need to see financial prosperity in the leadership to be able to convince the congregation of the message.

- The wrath of God against sin and the coming judgement are rarely mentioned in their messages (Romans 2:5; 1 Peter 4:5).

- Repentance is very rarely mentioned. Occasionally they may mention forgiveness, but they will give very little explanation of the repentance that is required to follow Jesus (Matthew 4:17; Mark 6:12; Acts 2:38).

- Finances are described as a seed that should be sown to reap an economic harvest, even though the Bible declares that the seed is the word of God and the harvest is righteousness and the souls of people (Luke 8:11, Isaiah 55:10-11).

- Tithing is seen as essential for true believers and without it, you would never experience God's blessings.

## What can we do about preachers that preach the prosperity gospel?
### - Pray for them
Some that preach a prosperity doctrine are just generally deceived themselves, while others willfully deceive people. Either way, we need to pray for them, that they would repent of their ways and lead others to the truth. But our prayers should not end there, we need to also pray for the many people who are being influenced by their false teachings regarding money.

In our prayers, let us remember that God can change even the toughest heart; He can lead to freedom for those that are in great bondage; He can set people free from demons, cults and false teachings.

### - Avoid them

If a prosperity teacher continues to teach what is biblically proven false, they are a false teacher. Preachers that persist in teaching a false doctrine or gospel like the prosperity gospel, should be avoided. While this may seem unloving and tough, it is biblical. Many Scriptures urge us to stay away from false teachers and prophets. Romans 16 seems to almost point directly at prosperity teachers, brethren that are teaching to feed their greed, lust and appetites.

> *'Now I urge you, brethren, keep your eye on those who cause dissensions and hindrances contrary to the teaching which you learned, and **turn away** them.* [18] *For such men are slaves, not of our Lord Christ but of their own appetites; and by their smooth and flattering speech they deceive the hearts of the unsuspecting.'*
> Romans 16:17-18

In verse 17, 'turn away' is also translated as 'avoid'. This Scripture describes those that are causing dissensions and hindrances as 'slaves, not of our Lord Christ but of their own appetites'. Prosperity preachers could be described as slaves of their own appetites. They preach and testify to always getting more, they pray and petition to receive more.

> *'I wrote you in my letter not to associate with immoral people;* [10] *I did not at all mean with the immoral people of this world, or with the covetous and*

> swindlers, or with idolaters, for then you would have to go out of the world. ¹¹ But actually, I wrote to you not to associate with any so-called brother if he is an immoral person, **or covetous**, or an idolater, or a reviler, or a drunkard, or a swindler—not even to eat with such a one. ¹² For what have I to do with judging outsiders? Do you not judge those who are within the church?'
> 1 Corinthians 5:9-12

The Greek word for covetous is 'pleonektēs' and means 'one desirous of having more'. The desire to have more is the common theme of the prosperity gospel.

### - Do not give money to them

As discussed earlier, the Bible tells us to never give under compulsion.

> 'Each one must do just as he has purposed in his heart, not grudgingly or under compulsion, for God loves a cheerful giver.'
> 2 Corinthians 9:7

Prosperity preaching compels us to financially give; most sermons given before the offering are designed to compel us to give. Even though the compulsion may be very subtle and most preachers would deny compelling people, the flavour of their message will compel you to give so that you don't miss out on God's blessings, or on God's return.

I would recommend that if you're feeling compelled to give, don't give to the one compelling you, but instead give what you have purposed in your heart secretly to someone in need, as directed by the Bible.

> 'Beware of practicing your righteousness before men to be noticed by them; otherwise you have no reward with your Father who is in heaven.
> ² So when you give to the poor, do not sound a trumpet before you, as the hypocrites do in the synagogues and in the streets, so that they may be honored by men. Truly I say to you, they have their reward in full. ³ But when you give to the poor, do not let your left hand know what your right hand is doing, ⁴ so that your giving will be in secret; and your Father who sees what is done in secret will reward you.'
> Matthew 6:1-4

## - Expose them

This point may not sit comfortably with many, and I understand that not everyone may be called to expose false teachers. It is important to understand that exposing false teachers is not necessarily an act of rebelliousness. Just look at Paul, he exposed people to bring about truth and freedom.

> 'For there are many rebellious men, empty talkers and deceivers, especially those of the circumcision, ¹¹ who must be silenced because they are upsetting whole families, teaching things they should not teach for the

> sake of sordid gain. ¹² One of themselves, a prophet of their own, said, "Cretans are always liars, evil beasts, lazy gluttons."'
> Titus 1:10-12

Today there may be some that expose false teachers with a wrong attitude, that being rebellion and unforgiveness. However, some are being biblical, with the motive and desire to bring about the truth and see them set free. The latter would be being obedient to the Bible by exposing false teachers and their doctrine.

Some may believe that it is best to keep the peace and not do anything to expose the false teachings of the prosperity doctrine. Yet look at the following Scriptures and see how Paul exposed and publicly named some that deserted him and turned away from sound doctrine.

> 'You are aware of the fact that all who are in Asia turned away from me, among whom are Phygelus and Hermogenes.'
> 2 Timothy 1:15

> 'Demas, having loved this present world, has deserted me and gone to Thessalonica; Crescens has gone to Galatia, Titus to Dalmatia.'
> 2 Timothy 4:10

*'keeping faith and a good conscience, which some have rejected and suffered shipwreck in regard to their faith. [20] Among these are Hymenaeus and Alexander, whom I have handed over to Satan, so that they will be taught not to blaspheme.'*
1 Timothy 1:19-20

*'their talk will spread like gangrene. Among them are Hymenaeus and Philetus, [18] men who have gone astray from the truth saying that the resurrection has already taken place, and they upset the faith of some.'*
2 Timothy 2:17-18

**The Old Testament too has warnings about those that teach to fulfil their greed:**

*'Son of man, prophesy against the shepherds of Israel. Prophesy and say to those shepherds, 'Thus says the Lord God, "Woe, shepherds of Israel who have been feeding themselves! Should not the shepherds feed the flock? [3] You eat the fat and clothe yourselves with the wool, you slaughter the fat sheep without feeding the flock. [4] Those who are sickly you have not strengthened, the diseased you have not healed, the broken you have not bound up, the scattered you have not brought back, nor have you sought for the lost; but with force and with severity you have dominated them."'*
Ezekiel 34:2-4

> 'And the dogs are greedy, they are not satisfied.
> And they are shepherds who have no understanding;
> They have all turned to their own way,
> Each one to his unjust gain, to the last one.
> [12] "Come," they say, "let us get wine, and let us drink heavily of strong drink;
> And tomorrow will be like today, only more so."'
> Isaiah 56:11-12

Ezekiel and Isaiah were just two of the Old Testament prophets that God used verbally to warn leaders about serving their own desires and greed. This continues into the New Testament, with warnings against covetousness and blessings for contentment.

## 15. Covetousness versus contentment

I could not think of a better way to conclude this book than with a chapter on contentment. Contentment is being satisfied with what you have; it removes all the stress and striving to receive more.

Unlike the prosperity gospel which preaches covetousness (always seeking to receive something better and more); contentment finds joy and freedom in living satisfied with what you have.

**Covetousness is greed, contentment is freedom.** There is great freedom in contentment, as it stops us from striving to acquire more and lusting after material possessions. With contentment, you find sufficiency with what you have and a trust in God knowing that He is your provider.

Christians will often quote the Scripture from Philippians 4:19 whenever someone mentions trusting God as their provider.

*And my God will supply all your needs according to His riches in glory in Christ Jesus.*
*Philippians 4:19*

While this verse can be used as an encouragement for us to trust God, it is based around the context of contentment. Without contentment, this verse can be used to almost blackmail God into giving us what we covet.

Just a few verses before it, there is another famously misquoted verse.

*I can do all things through Him who strengthens me.*
*Philippians 4:13*

This verse is often taken out of context and misquoted, to encourage us to strive towards, believe and achieve our dreams, our destiny and our desires.

Looking at the verses surrounding these two will help bring them into context and discover that it is about contentment. That we can be content in all situations and circumstances, knowing that in God we have sufficient for all our needs.

**Not that I speak from want, for I have learned to be content in whatever circumstances I am.**
*12 I know how to get along with humble means, and I also know how to live in prosperity; in any and every circumstance I have learned the secret of being filled and going hungry, both of having abundance and suffering need. 13 I can do all things through Him who strengthens me. 14 Nevertheless, you have done well to share with me in my affliction.*
*15 You yourselves also know, Philippians, that at the first preaching of the gospel, after I left Macedonia, no church shared with me in the matter of giving and receiving but you alone; 16 for even in Thessalonica you sent a gift more than once for my needs. 17 Not that I seek the gift itself, but I seek for the profit which*

> *increases to your account. <sup>18</sup> But I have received everything in full and have an abundance; I am amply supplied, having received from Epaphroditus what you have sent, a fragrant aroma, an acceptable sacrifice, well-pleasing to God. <sup>19</sup> And my God will supply all your needs according to His riches in glory in Christ Jesus.*
> *Philippians 4:11-19*

With contentment you don't need to strive to make more money, you no longer need to be focused on money.

> *Do not store up for yourselves treasures on earth, where moth and rust destroy, and where thieves break in and steal. <sup>20</sup> But store up for yourselves treasures in heaven, where neither moth nor rust destroys, and where thieves do not break in or steal;* **<sup>21</sup>for where your treasure is, there your heart will be also.**
> *Matthew 6:19-21*

Where is your heart? Is it focused on God or distracted by money? The problem with an over-emphasis on money is that it becomes the thing you love, and the love of money is the root to all sorts of evil. I have heard that money is not the root to all sorts of evil, but the love of money is. But again, we find that the verse quoted when put in context is about contentment.

*If anyone advocates a different doctrine and does not agree with sound words, those of our Lord Jesus Christ, and with the doctrine conforming to godliness, ⁴ he is conceited and understands nothing; but he has a morbid interest in controversial questions and disputes about words, out of which arise envy, strife, abusive language, evil suspicions, ⁵ and constant friction between men of depraved mind and deprived of the truth, who suppose that godliness is a means of gain.* **⁶ But godliness actually is a means of great gain when accompanied by contentment. ⁷ For we have brought nothing into the world, so we cannot take anything out of it either. ⁸ If we have food and covering, with these we shall be content**. *⁹ But those who want to get rich fall into temptation and a snare and many foolish and harmful desires which plunge men into ruin and destruction.* **¹⁰ For the love of money is a root of all sorts of evil**, *and some by longing for it have wandered away from the faith and pierced themselves with many griefs.*
*¹¹ But flee from these things, you man of God, and pursue righteousness, godliness, faith, love, perseverance and gentleness.*
1 Timothy 6:3-11

Sin always entangles us, and the love of money or covetousness after it is the root to all kinds of evil.

It was covetousness that entrapped Adam and Eve in the beginning. God had made them a perfect garden in a perfect world where they should have been content. Then one day, the serpent promised them something more, something better, and they coveted it, they reached out and took what they never should've taken. They were no longer content with what they had; they wanted the one thing they shouldn't have.

The love of money and the striving to get more is covetousness.

**Throughout Scripture, there are many warnings against covetousness, yet contentment is commanded and spoken of positively.**

*Make sure that your character is free from the love of money, being content with what you have; for He Himself has said, "I will never desert you, nor will I ever forsake you,"*
*Hebrews 13:5*

*No one can serve two masters; for either he will hate the one and love the other, or he will be devoted to one and despise the other. You cannot serve God and wealth.*

$^{25}$ *"For this reason I say to you, do not be worried about your life, as to what you will eat or what you will drink; nor for your body, as to what you will put on. Is not life more than food, and the body more than clothing? $^{26}$ Look at the birds of the air, that they do not sow, nor reap nor gather into barns, and yet your heavenly Father feeds them. Are you not worth much more than they? $^{27}$ And who of you by being worried can add a single hour to his life? $^{28}$ And why are you worried about clothing? Observe how the lilies of the field grow; they do not toil nor do they spin, $^{29}$ yet I say to you that not even Solomon in all his glory clothed himself like one of these. $^{30}$ But if God so clothes the grass of the field, which is alive today and tomorrow is thrown into the furnace, will He not much more clothe you? You of little faith! $^{31}$ Do not worry then, saying, 'What will we eat?' or 'What will we drink?' or 'What will we wear for clothing?' $^{32}$ For the Gentiles eagerly seek all these things; for your heavenly Father knows that you need all these things. $^{33}$ But seek first His kingdom and His righteousness, and all these things will be added to you.*
Matthew 6:24-33

Are modern preachers who preach prosperity encouraging covetousness?
If they preach about any of these topics, then I believe the answer is *yes*:
- God desiring to prosper you financially

- Living your best life now
- You need more money
- If you are spiritual you will be financially rich
- Unlocking wealth promised to you

These are just some of the themes that have been taught through modern-day preaching, and it begs an answer to the fore mentioned question. Are modern preachers preaching covetousness?

Some would answer the question saying it depends on your motive; do you want it for greed or to advance God's kingdom? The problem is that God's kingdom is not like worldly kingdoms. Worldly kingdoms are built on wealth and power, God's kingdom is built on righteousness, faith, love, and compassion.

> *Jesus answered, "My kingdom is not of this world. If My kingdom were of this world, then My servants would be fighting so that I would not be handed over to the Jews; but as it is, My kingdom is not of this realm."*
> *John 18:36*

> *for the kingdom of God is not eating and drinking, but righteousness and peace and joy in the Holy Spirit.*
> *Romans 14:17*

*Blessed are the poor in spirit, for theirs is the kingdom of heaven.*
*Matthew 5:3*

**Prosperity preachers never seem to be content, and this disqualifies them from being elders or bishops.**

*'This is a faithful saying: If a man desires the position of a bishop, he desires a good work. ² A bishop then must be blameless, the husband of one wife, temperate, sober-minded, of good behavior, hospitable, able to teach; ³ not given to wine, not violent, not greedy for money, but gentle, not quarrelsome, <u>not covetous</u>;'*
*1 Timothy 3:1-3*

Maybe the question we all need to answer is not about preachers that preach covetousness but whether we are living content or with a constant and selfish desire to get more.

Our hope, our trust, our faith needs to be in God our Father, not in money, possessions, or wealth.

Let us discover and enjoy the freedom of being content.

Let us discover the joy of anonymous generous giving, for surely this is the biblical way.

www.ingramcontent.com/pod-product-compliance
Lightning Source LLC
Chambersburg PA
CBHW050436010526
44118CB00013B/1547